Birthday Parties
Around the World

Birthday Parties

Around the World

by BARBARA RINKOFF

illustrated by Doug Anderson

M. BARROWS AND COMPANY, INC.
Distributed by William Morrow & Co., Inc., New York, 1967

To my dear mother, Sophia Frank Rich,
whose interest in people of foreign lands
has always inspired my own

Acknowledgements

I WOULD like to thank the following people for their invaluable help in collecting this information about their respective countries: Mollie Schick, Audree Shaw, Elisa Jacobs, Ricardo Frischtak, Georgina Dominguez, Jasper Jargil, Dorothy Silo, Catherine Tarride, Elfriede Brand, Greti Shemin, Didi Rebish, Patricia Collins, Myra Dromi, Eunice Welber, Mary Caruso, Helen Ranger, Michela Bartone, Jean Strasberger, Olga Salvato, Marjorie Duck, Emma Mead, Charlotte West, Marguerite Erler, Laura Flewellyn, Merly Laygo, Cathie O'Hara, Maria Anderson, Arne Mortenson, Rosemary Healy, Doloris Adendorff, and Zoya Voinov.

Contents

Introduction

"I want a birthday party that's different!" Sound familiar? After the novelty of the first few years of birthday parties, most children begin to want some special excitement connected with their celebrations. Mother has to come up with a novel idea to make the party different. But, she soon finds that it can't be a Princess party, because Lynn had one last year, or it can't be an Astronaut party, because Jimmy did it first. No matter what she thinks up, someone in the neighborhood has beaten her to it.

With my two sons, I settled for any new games that I could scout up, varying them with a supper party, movie party, or bowling party. But when my daughter, June, arrived at the "I want something different" stage, I had about exhausted my repertoire.

Frankly, I was sick of the same old thing, too. Then, one day, June asked, "How do children in other countries celebrate their birthdays?" She had me stumped, and her questions went on and on. "Why do I have candles on my cake? How did birthday parties start? What do other children eat for special treats? Do they play the same games we do?"

My own curiosity was aroused. I began to search into the whys and wherefores of the birthday celebration. I read whatever I could find, learning that the story of how birthday customs grew was fairly easy to locate, if you wanted to plow through a number of encyclopedias, but that up-to-date information on birthday customs, games, decorations, and food was unobtainable, even from information services at the United Nations. By now I was so fascinated that I began a series of personal interviews with United Nations personnel, foreign exchange students, overseas pen-pals, and recent immigrants to find out how birthdays are celebrated around the world today.

I learned about so many interesting customs, new games, and fresh ideas for decorations and party foods that we could hardly wait to try them out. It was exciting and fun to plan June's next birthday party. She and her friends were delighted with the new favors and different games. At the end of her two-hour party, no one wanted to leave and the children all pleaded for "Just one more game."

In this book I have set down all the information that

I had such fun gathering. I submit it along with the relieved remark of a friend: "At last, it's all there in one place!" And so, Happy Birthday and a good time to all . . . including Mother!

B.R.

International Mail Order Shopping for Birthday Parties

PART OF the fascination of preparing this book was thumbing through the mail-order catalogues of firms that sell items from many countries around the world. Often, when I wanted to give a foreign birthday party, I used to be held back by the thought of difficulties involved. I'd find myself thinking—an old-fashioned American party sounds great, but I haven't the time to make that old-fashioned candy. Or, I don't have the makings of that 12-year candle for the German party. Who sells Japanese lanterns? Italian candy? Exotic teas? Cake charms? English biscuits? I found all the answers in mail-order catalogues.

Once you become addicted to these international salesmen, you will find not only birthday items but many assorted sundries that you suddenly feel you cannot possibly live without. Their fascinating pages contain everything from exotic foods to unusual cake pans and molds to noodle-cutting machines like the one Grandma used to own to wonderfully original party decorations and gifts. Before long you end up sharpening your pencil to order something. And the anticipation is half the fun of mail-order shopping.

Many catalogues are available from all over the United States and many foreign countries. I have limited the list in the Directory on page 191 to a few of the best that contain items pertinent to birthday parties. As you read about each country in this book, you can refer to the list and check where to purchase teas for your Japanese party, cake charms for the English birthday cake, Italian candy, Danish cookies, party favors for a Scottish celebration, German seven-layer cake, records of circle dances for an Israeli party, Swiss lollypops, foreign dolls, tart pans, and so on and on. Many more foods, decorations, favors, games, utensils, and supplies than I have had room to mention are available through these catalogues, but just reading through the Directory will give you many ideas of your own.

The Story of Birthday Customs

BIRTHDAY parties began many, many years ago, in Europe. People believed in good and evil spirits in those days. Sometimes they called them good and evil fairies. They thought that the spirits gathered especially around a person who was celebrating his birthday. Everyone was afraid of these spirits and that they would cause harm to the birthday celebrant, and so he was surrounded by friends and relatives whose good wishes, and very presences, would protect him against the unknown dangers that the birthday held. The earlier after the break of day that good wishes and greetings were given, the sooner the birthday celebrant was given protection against the evil spirits. Giving gifts, along with good wishes, brought even greater protection. Eating together provided a further safeguard and helped to bring the blessings of the good spirits, godmothers, and wealthy relatives. So, the birthday gathering or party, along with its gifts and greetings, was originally intended to make a person safe from evil and to insure a good year to come.

In very early days, only kings or prominent men were thought important enough to celebrate their birthdays. But as time went on, the common people began to celebrate theirs, and eventually children's birthdays began to be celebrated most of all. The Germans were the first to celebrate children's birthdays with a party, called a *Kinderfeste* or children's festival.

Even the smallest child knows that birthday candles are to wish on. But why? The reason goes back to the early Greeks and Romans who thought that tapers or candles had magical qualities. They would offer prayers and make wishes to be carried up to the gods by the flames of candles. The gods would then send down their blessings and perhaps answer the prayers. The Germans were also the first to use lighted candles on birthday cakes. The birthday celebrant made a secret wish on the flame, just as most American children do today, and this wish might be granted IF all the candles were blown out with ONE puff. It became the custom to have one candle for each year of life and in some countries another candle "to grow on" has been added.

Playing games at birthday parties started a long

time ago as a symbolic wiping out of the past year and the starting of the new year ahead. Games of skill or strength were played and they were considered trials to show how much progress the birthday child had made in the past year. Everyone was proud as he demonstrated how much stronger and wiser he had become and how much more he had learned to do since his last celebration.

Giving birthday spanks is meant to insure good luck for the coming year. This custom has come down to us from very long ago and is still well known in many countries. It takes various forms (there are whacks, smacks, spanks, pinches, pricks, bumps), but all are given for good luck. If your child complains about friends following this age-old custom on his birthday you can explain that they are really wishing him well for the year to come.

Among the European peasantry, especially in Germany, the custom of planting a birth tree was practiced. People believed that a tree planted in honor of a child's birth had a mysterious connection with his welfare all his life. If the tree did well, the child would have good fortune; if the tree withered, or was cut down, or died, the child might be affected. Even today, in certain districts of Switzerland an apple tree is planted when a boy is born, a pear tree is planted for the birth of a girl. Sometimes an already grown tree is acclaimed the child's tree at his birth. Planting the birth tree is still a living practice in many countries of the South Pacific, in various parts of Africa, and among certain North American Indians. The custom is also noted in folk tales of England, France, Germany, Italy, and Russia.

Many superstitions are connected with the birthday. Astrologers, numerologists, and geomancers still use the date, hour, and place of birth as clues to good or bad fortune and they are firm believers in lucky and unlucky days. Each month, too, has its own birth stone, and many people believe that if this stone is worn by the person who was born in that month it will bring good luck.

January	Garnet
February	Amethyst
March	Aquamarine, bloodstone, or jasper
April	Diamond or sapphire
May	Emerald, agate, chalcedony, or carnelian
June	Pearl, moonstone, chalcedony, agate, or emerald
July	Ruby, onyx, carnelian, or turquoise
August	Sardonyx, chrysolite, or carnelian
September	Sapphire or chrysolite
October	Opal, tourmaline, aquamarine, or beryl
November	Topaz
December	Turquoise, lapis lazuli, or ruby

In some countries, birthday cakes are still used to tell fortunes. A ring or thimble, button or coin, or several small things of this type, is placed in the batter before the cake is baked. When the cake is sliced, your fortune is told according to the object found in your slice. If you find a ring you will marry some day. A thimble shows that you will be an old maid or a bachelor. A button indicates that you will be poor. A coin promises that you will be wealthy.

Each month has a special flower. If you want to bring a bouquet as a birthday gift, you could bring the flower that is associated with the month of the birthday.

January	Carnation
February	Violet
March	Jonquil
April	Daisy
May	Lilly-of-the-valley
June	Rose
July	Larkspur
August	Gladiolus
September	Aster
October	Calendula
November	Chrysanthemum
December	Narcissus

Poetry, too, has come down to us describing the future prospects of the child born on each day of the week.

Monday's child is fair of face,
Tuesday's child is full of grace,
Wednesday's child is dour and sad,
Thursday's child is merry and glad,
Friday's child is loving and giving,
Saturday's child must work for a living,
While the child that is born on the Sabbath Day
Is blithe and loving and good and gay.

Each month of the year has certain character traits associated with it.

January	Constancy
February	Sincerity
March	Courage
April	Innocence
May	Success in love
June	Health and longevity
July	Contentment
August	Married happiness or friendship
September	Clear thinking
October	Hope
November	Fidelity
December	Prosperity

In some countries, when a child is born, at least one of his given names is a saint's name. Throughout the calendar year, each day is a Saint's Name Day. (In fact, there are so many saints to be commemorated in history and folklore that several saints are associated with almost every day.) A child may be named after a saint on whose day he is born, in which case his birthday and his Saint's Name Day fall on the same date. Or he may be named after some other favorite saint, so that his birthday and his Saint's Name Day fall on different dates. In some countries, people celebrate only their Saint's Name Day, in other places only the birthday, and in still others both dates are occasions to be celebrated.

Birthday customs vary somewhat from one region to another within the same country. They are affected by religious differences, rural and urban differences, and economic status. But if you were invited, today, to a birthday party given in any of the countries I have written about in this book, you might expect to find children and their families celebrating very much as I have described.

Old-Fashioned American Parties

IN THE days of our great-grandparents, children looked forward to their birthdays as much as children do today. Perhaps the presents were not as grand, nor was as much fuss made over the children, but they did enjoy their celebrations.

The house might be decorated with flowers and the table set with linen or perhaps doily place settings. A frosted layer cake served as the birthday cake. The Happy Birthday song has been traditional for generations, as have been the secret wish before blowing out the candles and the serving of the first slice to the birthday child. Sandwiches, doughnuts, crullers, spice cakes, tapioca, custard, fruit or jam tarts, pies, or gingerbread men might be served as well as the cake. Caramels, rock candy, glazed almonds, candied peels, roast chestnuts, popcorn, fruit, cinnamon sticks, lemon drops, red hots, licorice twists, gum drops, and fudge were popular sweets. (Many old-fashioned candies are still made commercially; see Mail Order Shopping Directory.) A molasses-candy pull was sometimes the high point of the party. If there was enough snow outside, the children in the family had fun making a homemade frozen mousse to serve at the celebration. Fruit punch was a favorite drink.

Glazed Almonds

1–1¼ cups almonds   1 cup sugar
   1 cup water

Heat the water and sugar together until the sugar is completely dissolved (about 6 minutes). Lay in the nuts carefully, not putting in more than 12 at a time. Boil very gently until tender. Remove carefully with a slotted spoon, one piece at a time, and drain on absorbent paper. Sprinkle more sugar over the nuts, turning them to be sure sugar coats all sides. Dry slowly in the sun or in a cool oven. Keep in a closely covered metal container.

Pulled Molasses Candy

3 tablespoons butter   ⅔ cup sugar
2 cups molasses   ¼ cup vinegar

Melt butter in kettle, add molasses and sugar, and stir to dissolve sugar. Bring to boiling point, and boil slowly for 3 minutes without stirring. Then stir constantly until mixture reaches the hard-crack stage (290°F. on a candy thermometer), from 6 to 10 minutes after boiling begins. Now add vinegar, remove from fire, stir well, and pour into well-greased pan or dish.

As soon as the candy is cool enough to handle, take whole mass and pull it out as far as possible with lightly buttered hands. Pull again and again until candy is light yellow and porous (about 10 minutes). Don't squeeze and handle as lightly as possible. When it is of correct consistency and color, pull into long strands of desired thickness and cut into 1-inch lengths with greased scissors. Lay on greased plates or baking sheet to harden. Makes about 1¼ pounds. Takes about 45 minutes to complete.

Candied Lemon or Orange Peel

The outside of the peel should be thoroughly washed before the fruit is peeled. Drop peel into salted water (1–2 tablespoons salt to 1 quart water), and let stand for 24 hours.

Drain, cover with cold water, bring to boiling point, and repeat until there is no salty taste (3–4 waters). Boil gently in fresh water until skin is very tender. Then drain again, and scrape inside lightly with a spoon to remove loose part of white. Cut peel with scissors into strips $\frac{1}{4}$ to $\frac{1}{2}$ inch wide and 1 to 2 inches long.

Weigh peel, measure out equal weight of sugar, and for each cup of sugar add $1\frac{1}{2}$ cups water. Boil sugar and water together for 10 minutes, then add peel. Simmer until syrup is almost absorbed (10 to 15 minutes). Turn peel often with a fork while cooking. Let cook in syrup, then reheat a little and lift with a silver fork to a plate covered with granulated sugar. Roll in sugar and spread on waxed paper to dry. Takes about 2 hours. Keep in airtight container.

Caramels

2 cups sugar	3 tablespoons butter
1 cup light or dark corn syrup	$\frac{1}{4}$ teaspoon salt
3 cups milk	1 teaspoon vanilla
	1 cup chopped nuts

Cook together sugar, corn syrup, and 1 cup of the milk until mixture forms a soft ball when a little is dropped into a cup of cold water. Then add another cup of milk and cook again until soft-ball stage. Add last cup of milk, and butter and salt, and cook a third time to soft-ball stage. Then stir in vanilla and nuts, and pour onto buttered pan. Let stand for 6 hours, then cut into squares.

13

Strawberry Mousse

1 quart fresh strawberries or 1 package frozen strawberries	1 egg white
	Fine granulated sugar
	½ teaspoon vanilla
1 pint cream	Rock salt

Hull and crush the fresh strawberries, or thaw and crush the frozen berries. Whip cream, and beat egg white stiff. Fold together lightly cream, egg white, and strawberries, and add fine granulated sugar to taste and vanilla.

Pour the mousse into a metal canister with a tightly fitting lid, and tie a folded dish towel firmly around the edge of the lid. Dig a hole in a snowbank and line it with rock salt. Put the canister in the hole, pack it down firmly with snow, and leave it to freeze for several hours. Lacking a snowbank, freeze mousse, covered with waxed paper, in a deep refrigerator tray for 3 hours with the controls set at "very cold." Serves six.

Fruit Punch

2 cups sugar	1 cup pineapple juice
1 quart cold water	1 cup orange juice
½ cup lemon juice	

Boil together sugar and water for 10 minutes. Add fruit juices and chill. Dilute with a little ice water and serve with ice cubes.

Grape Fizz

Mix together 1 quart ginger ale and 1 quart grape juice, and pour into glasses with crushed ice.

Grapefruit Fizz

Mix together 1 quart ginger ale and 1 pint grapefruit juice, and pour into glasses with crushed ice.

Party favors have become much more necessary to an American birthday party than they ever were in the old days when children might never have heard of such a thing. An idea for party hats for an "old-fashioned" party today might be inexpensive stocking caps from the Five-and-Ten for the boys and cotton-print "Grandma" sunbonnets for the girls. (One mail-order source for sunbonnets, Old Country Store, The Nashville House, Nashville, Indiana.) Homemade "lace" paper doilies (white on a colored paper table cloth, or colored on a white cloth) will make a great display on the party table.

Lace-paper Doilies

Fold a circular piece of paper in half. Then fold in half again; once again, and once again. Then cut small shapes out of the folded sides and the wide end of the paper. When the paper is unfolded, a lovely snowflake design will appear.

Usually, expensive gifts were not given to children on their birthdays. A handmade memento from a friend was a welcome present. Fruits, nuts, or candy were given by the family, sometimes accompanied by a new outfit or something useful the child really needed. If the birthday child were to receive money as a gift from his parents, it might be hidden about the house or grounds and he then had to treasure hunt for it.

GAMES

A NUMBER of the games played by girls and boys several generations ago are still played today: Hide and Seek, Pin the Tail on the Donkey, Blindman's Buff, Jacks and Ball, Tag (see Game Directory), relay races, and such things as playing marbles, kite flying, leap frog, blowing bubbles, spinning tops, and puppet shows could all be part of a birthday party.

Some old-fashioned games that could be revived today would be horseshoe pitching, rolling hoops, broad-jumping contests, ninepins (bowling), husking bees, shuffleboard, and, weather permitting, snowman sculpture contests. Mothers today may not be up to facing some of the old games with a frontier flavor such as races to catch a well-greased pig, wrestling contests, and wood-chopping contests. The Game Directory on page 179 lists other familiar games that American children have known for a long time.

And of course, children have always loved to be excused from their chores and allowed to stay up later than usual. A birthday is still the best possible excuse for these special treats.

Australia

BECAUSE of the vast distances between homes and the difficulty of transportation in many parts of Australia, children often have a school luncheon party during recess so that the birthday child can celebrate with school friends who ordinarily could not join him at home. But when neighbors do live nearby, the party is held at home.

Australia's warm climate leads to outdoor celebrations. For younger children's parties, the back yard is decorated with balloons and streamers and the party table is festively set with colored paper plates and napkins. A fancy party hat and an inexpensive favor is placed at each setting. The birthday child's chair is at the head of the table and is sometimes decorated, too.

Older girls and boys usually enjoy a barbecue party. Chops and sausages cooked on an outdoor grill are Australian favorites.

Food is abundant, with sausage rolls, sandwiches, Hundreds and Thousands (colored sugar sprinkles) on buttered bread, jelly (any type of gelatin dessert), ice cream, peanuts, and candy such as jelly beans, chocolates, and licorice allsorts* being served besides the birthday cake. The first slice of cake goes to the birthday child. Homemade marshmallows set into ice-cream cups are also great favorites. And most children's parties are not complete without raspberry vinegar, which we know as the old-fashioned drink, raspberry shrub.

Raspberry Shrub

5 quarts fresh raspberries	Sugar
1 quart mild vinegar	Cloves

Pour vinegar over raspberries and let stand for 24 hours. Strain and measure liquid. Add ½ pound of sugar for each quart of juice. Bring to a boil, cool, and pour into bottles. To add flavor, put in 1 dozen cloves when the juice is heated. To serve, pour syrup into tall glass with ice, and add water or soda water.

---

* These are licorice candies of different shapes and colors. Some are filled candies, with licorice on the outside; still others are all licorice with colored beads of sugar on them. They can be purchased under this name at Macy's, Herald Square, New York City.

Sausage Rolls

A thin pastry dough (use a mix if you want) is wrapped around already cooked cocktail-size sausages. They are then baked until the pastry is golden brown, and served hot.

Australian Sultana Loaf
(Raisin Loaf)

Tastes better on the second day and keeps for four or five days, if it will last that long!

½ cup mashed potato	½ teaspoon salt
½ cup sugar	½ cup raisins
2 cups flour	1 cup milk
2 teaspoons baking powder	½ teaspoon cinnamon
	¼ teaspoon nutmeg

¼ teaspoon powdered ginger

Glazing for top:

3 teaspoons confectioners sugar	1½ teaspoons hot water

Place potato and sugar in a bowl and beat together. Sift together flour, baking powder, and salt. Combine with potato mixture. Stir in raisins, then add the milk and spices, and beat well. Pour into a greased loaf tin, and bake in a preheated 325°F. oven for 1 hour. Let cool. To glaze the top, mix the sugar with the hot water, and spread over the cooled cake.

Australian children love minature toy ornaments on their party cakes. A fairy ballet dancer; nursery-rhyme character, football or cricket bat and the like decorate the birthday cake, which is a fruitcake iced in a pastel color. There are candles on it, one for each year, and the birthday child makes a secret wish and blows them out. Happy Birthday, or Happy Birthday to ——(name)——, is likely to appear on the top of the cake, too. The guests at the party count out the age of the birthday child with claps, one for each year and one for luck. The birthday song is the same as the one sung in the United States. Gifts of books, hair ribbons, and toys are the most popular in Australia.

Party Hat

USE A rectangular piece of colored paper. Fold it in half at the middle of the long side. Place a mark at the center of the folded edge. Fold down this edge into two triangles starting from the center mark; the triangles will not extend to the bottom of the paper. Now fold the first extending edge at the bottom up over the triangles; fold the other edge up over the other side. Fold the corners of the turned-up edges back over the two bottom points of the hat, and glue or stample them. Add a feather—a real feather or one cut out of a different color paper—to the side of the hat for decoration. Or add a paper flower. You could have hats with feathers for boys and flowers for girls.

GAMES

A HANKIE, miniature toy, or a chocolate are favorite prizes for game winners.

Magic Parcel
(see Musical Parcels, page 53)

This game can cause great excitement among the five- to seven-year-old crowd.

Postman's Knock

One child is selected as Postman. The other children come up to him and say "What is there today, Mr. Postman?" He turns and chases them. When he catches someone, that person must kiss him as a penalty, and then that child becomes Postman.

Drop the Handkerchief
(see Game Directory)

Oranges and Lemons

Played like London Bridge and ends in a Tug-of-War (see Game Directory).

Hide and Seek
(see Game Directory)

Treasure Hunt
(see Game Directory)

At school, the birthday child sits at the front of his class, Happy Birthday is sung to him by his classmates, and his age is clapped out by the children. In Sunday school, the birthday child sits in a special chair and he is allowed to pass the collection basket. He is served his favorite foods at dinner on the evening of his birthday. The twenty-first birthday is a big event in Australia and often an elaborate party is held in a hired hall to celebrate that the child is now officially an adult.

Belgium

GELUKKIG VERJAARDAG (Happy Birthday) is the Flemish greeting. Belgian children who speak French say *Bon Anniversaire*. As soon as the birthday child awakens he has to be on the look-out, because his family tries to catch him unawares and prick him with a needle, for luck.

The family decorates the house with flowers for the party, and the table is set with good linen and china. *Halo* (Hello) the birthday child greets his guests, and he says *Merci* (Thank you) as they give him their gifts of toys, games, or candy.

The children are served petits-fours, French pastries, cookies, Belgian pralines (chocolate candies filled with fruits, nuts, or flavored liquids), and soda or hot cocoa. The birthday cake is round and covered with butter-cream frosting. The birthday greeting is piped in colored icing across the top and candles, one for each year, circle the cake. Or the cake may be frosted with whipped cream and a little flag with Happy Birthday written on it is stuck in the center. The birthday child in Belgium also makes a secret wish and blows the candles out, and he receives the first slice of the cake. The birthday song is the same as the one sung in the United States and, since World War II, it is sung in English.

Petits-Fours

Pound cake   Vegetable coloring
White frosting (below)

Cut the pound cake into small cubes. Dip each cube in the frosting so that it is completely covered, then place it on a cake rack. Decorate the tops with a tiny flower made from colored icing, or use candied cherries, nuts, chocolate sprinkles, etc. Leave the cakes on the rack until the frosting is set.

White frosting for petits-fours:

⅔ cup sugar   3 tablespoons cold
 1 egg white   water

Mix the ingredients together in the top of a double boiler. Cook for 5 minutes over boiling water. Remove from the heat and dip the cakes in the frosting before it sets.

A few quiet games like dominos are sometimes played at Belgian birthday parties, but ordinarily games are not organized. The birthday child's special privileges are to have his favorite foods served, not to have to do his usual chores for the day, and to stay up later than his customary bedtime. Sometimes his parents take him on a day's outing instead of giving him a party. The twenty-first birthday is considered the most important in Belgium, too, and signifies that the child is now officially grown-up.

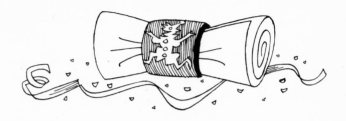

Brazil

AT MOST Brazilian birthday parties, food is served buffet style. The children sit on chairs or on the floor and eat from plates which they hold in their laps. These are afternoon parties. Relatives visit that evening to celebrate with the family.

The birthday child greets his guests with *Como vai?* (How are you?). They in turn wish him *Feliz Aniversário* (Happy Birthday) and give him their gifts. The birthday child responds with *Muito obrigado* (Much obliged).

The party buffet table is laden with food and stacks of paper plates and napkins with a birthday picture or Happy Birthday in Portugese printed on them. Wooden or cardboard napkin rings decorated with a design or a fairy-tale character (Cinderella, etc.) are used to hold the napkins. If cardboard rings are used, the guests take them home as party favors. Balloons and streamers decorate the party room.

Napkin Rings

Cut strips of colored cardboard or construction paper 1½ inches wide and 7 inches long. Glue ends together. Cut small designs or figures from a different color paper, shiny metallic paper, or a patterned gift-wrapping paper, and glue on to decorate.

The birthday cake is large and round and is covered with a rich butter-cream icing. Happy Birthday to _____(name)_____ is written across the top of the cake and flowers made of icing decorate it. There are candles, one for each year, on the cake, and the birthday child makes a secret wish and blows them out. Ice-cream cake is also very popular as a birthday cake. It is usually made with thin layers of cake alternating with thick layers of variously flavored ice cream and is topped and edged with frozen whipped cream. Colorful homemade candies in pretty shapes (both chocolate and hard candies) and fancy hors d'oeuvres of all kinds are served. If the party is a birthday luncheon, there may be hot dogs with mustard and ketchup. Ice cream in some form is a must at Brazilian birthday parties, and Cokes are the favorite party drink.

Brazilian Dreams
(*Sonhos*)

LITTLE puffy pastries, crisp outside and hollow inside.

½ cup water
1½ teaspoons sugar
Pinch of salt
½ cup flour

2 eggs
Salad oil for deep frying
Powdered sugar and cin-
    namon, sifted together

Place the water, sugar, and salt in a saucepan, and bring to a boil. Add the flour, and stir quickly until the mixture forms a ball that doesn't separate. Remove from the stove and cool. Add an egg and beat the mixture with a spoon until smooth. Add the other egg, beating the mixture thoroughly. Now drop small balls of the dough from a teaspoon into deep hot oil. Take out when golden brown and drain on absorbent paper. Sprinkle with sifted powdered sugar and cinnamon.

The children all sing the birthday song to the birthday child. It has the same tune as the song that is sung in the United States although the words are different.

Parabens para voce,
Parabens para voce,
Muitas felicidades,
Muitos anos de vida!

Congratulations to you,
Congratulations to you,
Much happiness,
Many years of life!

GAMES

HERE ARE some of the games you might play if you were to attend a Brazilian birthday party. The first one is good for an indoor party:

Anel
(*Ring*)

The children form a circle and hold their hands behind their backs. One child is IT and stands inside the circle. Another child has a ring and passes around the outside of the circle pretending to give the ring to one of the children. He does finally give it to someone and IT has to guess who really got the ring. He may have three guesses (or more if there are very many children) and if he doesn't guess correctly he must pay a forfeit (see page 187).

Peteca

Some players become quite skilled at this. *Peteca* means a leather-covered trunk or bag; for the game, the bag is a small leather pouch full of sand, with feathers tied to the top. A bean bag will work well, too.

The bag is tossed up into the air by the first child to play, and with one hand he must hit it back up into the air over and over without letting it fall to the ground. As he does this, the child recites the alphabet. The player who can get through the most letters of the alphabet before missing the bag and letting it drop is the winner.

THIS is a lot of fun indoors or out:

Hit the Penny

A bamboo stick 12 to 18 inches long is set upright in the ground; a piece of broomstick may be substituted. On top of the stick is a coin, and the stick is in the center of a circle, about 3 feet in diameter, marked on the ground. If the game is played indoors, the coin can be placed on a stick propped in a Christmas-tree stand and the circle can be indicated by a string.

Players stand at a distance of 4 to 6 feet from the stick and take turns trying to knock the coin off the stick by throwing a penny at it. If they knock it off and outside the 3-foot circle, they score one point. If it drops inside the circle or if they miss it, they score nothing.

Boys become quite ingenious at this game:

Gato Doente
(*Sick Cat*)

The cat is IT. The cat tries to tag another player who must then hold the spot where he has been tagged while he becomes the Sick Cat and tries to tag someone.

Girls enjoy the confusion of this game and run about more like chickens without heads than rabbits.

Coelho na Toca
(*Rabbit in His House*)

Two children are paired off and hold hands. They are the house. A third child stands in front of them and they circle him by holding hands on the other side too. He is the rabbit. Several of these groups are formed. One extra rabbit is left; he is IT. At the signal of "Rabbit in his house," all the rabbits must duck out and find new homes. The extra rabbit also tries to find a home. The rabbit left homeless becomes IT.

GIRLS have a good time with this one, too:

Minha Direita Desocupada
(There's an empty place on my right)

Chairs are placed in a circle. One chair is left empty. Each player takes the name of a flower. The player to the left of the empty chair calls, "There's an empty place on my right. Come here (names a flower)!" If the child who has chosen this flower forgets his name and does not come and take the chair, he must pay a forfeit (see page 187).

A FAVORITE with boys and tomboys:

Luta de Galo
(Chicken Fight)

There are two players. Each player has a hankie stuck in his belt and folds his right arm across his chest. Each child must hop only on his right foot; the left foot cannot touch the ground. With the free left arm, each child tries to get his opponent's hankie. The opponent may ward off a blow with his right elbow but may not unbend his right arm.

THIS always causes the giggles:

Cabra-cega
(*Blind Goat*)

A blindfolded child touches another child's face to try to guess who it is.

Musical Chairs
(*see Game Directory*)

WATCH out for squabbles.

Pin the Tail on the Rabbit

Played the same way as our Pin the Tail on the Donkey (see Game Directory). Small children love this but are clever at peeking.

FOR OLDER players. Guessing games about information are often played in Brazil:

Name as many makes of cars as you can.
Name as many authors as you can.
Name as many countries as you can.

Apple on a String

Buck teeth are an asset! An apple is hung from a string. With both hands behind your back you must catch it in your mouth.

Morral
(*Grab Bag*)

Any number can play. Fill a bag with written instructions for stunts, enough for each child at the party. As each one draws his slip of paper, he must do his stunt. See the list of forfeits on page 187 for suggestions.

FOR VERY young children, making cut-outs and drawing pictures are always popular.

If balloons have been used to decorate the party room, they usually have been tied in a large cluster to the ceiling light. When the party is over, the children jump to catch a balloon for themselves. This is their prize at the party, because no prizes are given for winning games.

In Brazilian schools, the lower-grade classes sing the Happy Birthday song to the birthday child. He in turn brings cake and candy to treat his classmates. A special birthday privilege for a Brazilian child is staying up later than usual.

Between the ages of fifteen and eighteen, most Brazilian girls are given a debutante party on one of their birthdays. It is a large party to introduce the young lady to society, friends, and relatives of the family and to announce that she is officially grown-up.

Cuba

THE CUBAN birthday party is an all-out affair. The people celebrate in the most elaborate way they can afford and dress in their best clothes. Almost everybody is invited to the party—friends, relatives, neighbors, and teachers. In recent years, the custom has been to send out birthday invitations with an appropriate picture and verse. The house is decorated with balloons, streamers, and lots of flowers. If there is a garden or back yard, colored lights are strung there. When a family can afford it, a magician is hired to amuse the children or musicians come to play during the party. Sometimes the birthday child treats his friends to rides at an amusement park. Customarily Cuban children are allowed to stay home from school as a special birthday treat.

Paper Lantern

Use colored paper 9 inches long and 6 inches wide. Draw two lines ½ inch from each lengthwise edge. Then fold the paper in half lengthwise down the center. Now cut at ¼-inch intervals all along the folded edge down to the ½-inch mark opposite. Then paste the short sides of the paper together to form the lantern. Add a paper strip handle for hanging. Paper lanterns may be hung over strings of small colored lights but never over a strong bulb nor over a candle.

¡Hola! (Hello), the guests are greeted. They wish the birthday child *Feliz Cumpleaños* (Happy Birthday) and give him a gift, for which he responds, *Gracias* (Thank you). Small toys, books, and candy are the customary presents in Cuba. Colorful paper plates and napkins with Happy Birthday in Spanish or a design on them are used on the table. Small toys are given to each guest as party favors. The table is laden with good things to eat: bowls of chicken salad, little tamales, *pastelites* (little pies filled with meat, fish, or fruit), *cangrejitos* (small pies baked in the shape of crabs and filled with meat, fish, or seafood), fruits, cookies, candies, chocolate bonbons, and *mantecaditas* (like French pastries). Ice cream and Coke or fruit punch finish off the feast. The birthday cake is a layer cake frosted with chocolate or sugar icing, or sometimes it is covered with whipped cream. It is decorated with flowers

and *Felicidades a* ——<u>(name)</u>—— (Congratulations to ——<u>(name)</u>——) is written on the top. Often a standing decoration representing the child's hobby, such as a baseball player or a dancing doll, is placed on the cake. Circling it are the candles for each year of life. The Cuban birthday child makes the usual secret wish, blows the candles out, and is served the first slice of cake. The birthday song, in Spanish, is the same one that is sung in the United States.

Cuban Banana Sherbet

Pour 1 cup of powdered sugar over half a dozen very thinly sliced bananas, and set aside for 30 minutes. Then add 1 quart of water to dissolve the sugar. Add the grated rind of ½ a lemon and a little lemon juice to taste, and freeze.

GAMES

My Friend Has Returned from the Orient

The players divide into two opposing groups. A "safe" line is drawn a little distance away to the rear of each group.

The first group secretely decides on some object to act out in pantomime. The children then approach the other group and say, "My friend has returned from the Orient." The other group must then reply, "What did he bring with him?" The first group then acts out its pantomime (a bed, a car, a pot of stew, a stack of books, etc.).

When the members of the second team guess the answer, they immediately chase the first group, trying to capture as many players as they can for their side before the first group is able to reach its safe line. The game is repeated, this time with the other side doing the pantomime, and continues until one side has captured all the players of the other side.

SMALL children love this because they always "catch":

Fishing Game

A type of standing well is made, big enough so that an adult can hide inside and the children cannot see in. It can be made of cardboard. Each child fishes in the well with a fishing line that has a pin attached to it. When the line is lowered, the adult inside the well pins a small or funny gift onto the line for the child to pull out.

La Gallinita Ciega
(*The Blind Hen*)

Played like Blindman's Buff (see Game Directory).

El Rabo al Burro

This is our Pin the Tail on the Donkey (see Game
Directory).

Las Prendas
(*The Jewelry*)

This is the same game as *Anel* that is played in Brazil
(page 30).

Musical Chairs

A large room is needed for this version. It is played
like Musical Chairs in the United States, except that
the players march in a wide circle far from the chairs
and must run a good distance to get a chair when the
music stops (see Game Directory).

A prize of a toy or game that is more of a real gift
than the party favors is given to game winners.

The highlight of the Cuban birthday party is the
piñata that is hung from the ceiling. The old type of
piñata was a deep clay bowl filled with goodies. Each
child got a chance to break it open by whacking it
with a stick. A hollow papier-mâché *piñata* is more
usual today, made in an elaborate painted shape and
filled with small toys, hard candies, cookies, and chocolate bonbons. Ribbons hang from the *piñata* and each
child gets a chance to pull one. When the correct ribbon is pulled, the *piñata* opens and out spill all the

goodies for the children to share. The child who opened the *piñata* gets a special prize as a reward.

Piñata

Fill a large paper bag or colored-paper shopping bag with candies, small toys, cookies, etc. Staple or tape it firmly closed. Decorate it into an animal figure or strange shape with designs cut out of colored paper and pasted on, crêpe-paper curls, ribbons, etc., and hang it from the ceiling. The children take turns being blindfolded and trying to break open the bag by whacking it with a broom handle.

Small children are told stories at the birthday party, and some of the Cuban favorites are just the same as ours—*La Caperucita Roja* (Little Red Riding Hood), *Los Tres Osos* (The Three Bears).

The fifteenth birthday is very important to Cuban girls. At this time a girl is considered a young lady and no longer a child. She may now wear lipstick and high heels and she may invite boys to her house, though she may not go out on dates without a chaperon. The twenty-first birthday is important because this is the time that adulthood is legally recognized and the vote is given.

Denmark

WHEN the birthday child awakens on the morning of his birthday, he finds gifts from his family stacked around his bed. While he was still asleep, his parents placed the presents where he would see them as soon as he opened his eyes, and sometimes some are even stuffed under his pillow.

Everybody in the family gets up early to say *Tillykke* (To luck), or the more formal *Tillykke på Fødselsdagen* (Happy Birthday, or To luck on your birthday). After this, the child is presented with his birthday flag, a small cloth Danish flag that is his all day and is placed in front of him at the table. When anyone celebrates a birthday in Denmark, a flag is flown from a window outside the house. In the cities, when you look at an apartment house, you see many flags flying from the building any day of the week. Each flag stands for someone celebrating a birthday.

Danish Flag

Cut a piece of red paper 6 inches by 4 inches. Glue a strip of white paper ½ inch wide down the middle lengthwise. Then, 2 inches from the left-hand narrow edge, glue another white strip exactly at right angles to the first strip. Do the same on the other side of the flag, and trim the four ends of the white strips at the edges of the flag. Or you may paint the same design in red poster paint on white paper, leaving the two crossed stripes white.

Mount the flag at the left edge (at the short end of the white cross) on a thin applicator stick, or on a knitting needle, by rolling about ½ inch of the paper around the stick and gluing it. Push one end of the "flagpole" into a lump of clay to hold it upright.

A day or so before his party, the birthday child has given out party invitations to his friends. The invitations are picture cards with a little verse inviting the guests to the party, which is usually held in the afternoon. Relatives arrive in the evening to celebrate with the family and to present their gifts. Friends are greeted with *Hej!* (Hi, or Hello), and as each guest gives his gift to the birthday child he is told *Tak* (Thank you). Money is a common gift, from classmates, friends, and relatives, and the birthday cards sent by them have a birthday picture but with a message written by the sender, rather than a printed verse.

The house is not especially decorated for the party except possibly with balloons. Paper plates and napkins are used and the birthday child has his cloth Danish flag in front of his place. All the other guests have smaller paper flags at their places. A large round layer cake serves as the birthday cake. It is covered with colored icing or whipped cream, and the birthday child gets the first slice. Ice cream is very popular in Denmark, but ice cream cakes are not served at a birthday party. There is a candle for each year on the cake and the birthday child makes the traditional secret wish before blowing them out.

Boller is always served at a Danish birthday party. It is a sweet white bread, round as a ball, and is eaten with butter. It is baked by the child's mother especially for the party. Hot dogs are very popular at Danish parties, but they are longer and thinner and taste different from those in the United States. All types of chocolate and hard candies and cookies are served, hot cocoa with whipped cream is a must for the children, and *Sodavand* (soda) is also popular as a party drink.

GAMES

THIS game is a favorite with the boys. It is obviously best played outdoors, and have a bucket of water at hand—just in case!

Bird's Alive

Any number can play. The children are seated in a circle. They pass a lighted paper or stick from one to another. The player in whose hand the fire goes out must pay a forfeit (see page 187). They may blow on the paper or stick to keep alive any spark of fire, and as they pass the fire, they say, "Bird's alive!"

THIS is a good mixer game:

Pantelege

This word is used for all forfeit games, of which there are many types. In one type of *Pantelege,* a child is blindfolded. The other children each place an item belonging to them in a container. The blindfolded child picks out and holds up one of these articles, and then he tells the owner what he must do to redeem the article (see page 187).

Boys take this very seriously. Have your camera ready to catch the girls' excitement:

Stafetlo

This is the potato race we know in the United States. Two teams are set up. For each team there is a spoon, to be held with one hand, and there is a potato or hard-boiled egg in the spoon. The teams have a relay race and the egg or potato must not be dropped as the players run back and forth. If a player does drop the contents of his spoon, he must go back to the beginning of his relay and start over. The first team to complete all its relays wins the race.

THIS IS a mess—but they love it:

A child is blindfolded. He must then feed himself a gooey cake, ice cream, or the like. There is a variation that is even worse—but they enjoy it even more. Blindfold two children and have them feed each other. If you've lived through this, I congratulate you.

Pin the Tail on the Pig

Played like Pin the Tail on the Donkey (see Game Directory).

For OLDER girls and boys, guessing games about information are very popular at Danish birthday parties:

Name as many authors as you can.
Name as many flowers as you can.
Name as many inventions as you can.

Billedlotteri

This is a bingo game played with animal picture cards instead of numbers.

Smaller children love to hear a Hans Christian Andersen story at a party, and occasionally they make clay figures and a prize is given for the best one. Prizes are small toys or candy and they are also given to the children who win games. Party favors are not usual, but if balloons were used for decoration they are given to the children when they leave.

Classmates sing Happy Birthday to the birthday child in school. Lower grade teachers will read a Hans Christian Andersen story to the class in his honor, and he brings hard candy to treat his classmates and the teacher. His special privileges are to choose the dinner menu for the family and to stay up later than usual.

If the birthday party is for a teenage girl, the boys who are invited bring the hostess's mother flowers. The sixteenth birthday is very important to Danish boys because they are then allowed to drive a motor scooter.

England

ENGLISH birthday cakes often tell your fortune. Small charms are mixed into the batter before it is baked. When the cake is cut, your fortune is told according to the object found in your slice. A ring means you will marry; a thimble shows that you will be an old maid or a bachelor; a button indicates being poor; a coin promises wealth, and so on.

English children invite their friends to a birthday party at home by sending out invitations with a birthday picture and verse on them. Balloons, streamers, and the birthday cards that have been received decorate the house. The party table is colorful with paper plates and napkins, party hats, and crackers (snappers) at each place setting. Each guest receives a small noise-making toy, a party favor, and a balloon to take home.

Clothing, toys, money, sweets (candy), or almost anything the birthday child might enjoy are given as gifts.

Crackers

Use cardboard roll that toilet paper is wrapped around. Fill with candies and a small toy or charm. Wrap in birthday paper, tying each end with a ribbon. If you want a snapper so that the favor will make noise when it is opened, this can be bought (see Mail-Order Shopping Directory) and glued inside.

Up to the age of nine years, English children sit at the table for their refreshments. They are served sandwiches (egg, tomato, ham), sweet biscuits (cookies), small buns (rather like hotcross buns, made of sweet dough, they are round and soft, with currants inside, and have shiny tops), jellies (gelatin desserts), and fruit salad. Children ten or over are served buffet style and stand when they eat. Hot sausages, trifle, sandwiches, cookies, cakes, fruit salad, and biscuits (cheese crackers and the like) are enjoyed by the older children, and a small bar is also set up for them where they may get Cokes, orange and lemon (pure-fruit concentrates that are mixed with plain or carbonated water), and cider. A bowl of mixed sweets (candy) is set on the table at parties for either age group so that the children can help themselves.

The birthday cake for children under seven is an iced sponge cake. After the seventh year, the cake is an iced fruit cake in any shape and with any color of icing the birthday child wants. Some popular forms are the shape of the number of the birthday, a fan shape, or the form of a cottage, or a locomotive perhaps, as well as round or square cakes. Butter cream is used to ice the cake, Happy Birthday to ——(name)—— is written on the top, and candles, one for each year, also decorate it. Before the first slice is cut for him, the birthday child blows out the candles while the guests sing the birthday song (the same one as ours). There may be a home movie or a puppet show after the feast, in which case ice cream is served when the entertainment is over.

Trifle

Sponge cake, sliced thin	Stewed berries or fruit,
Milk	not too sweet nor too
Sugar	moist
Vanilla extract	

Custard Sauce:

4 egg yolks	2 cups milk
1 cup sugar	

To make the sauce, beat the yolks in the top of a double boiler. Beat in the sugar and milk. Then cook and stir over hot water, making a thickened golden sauce. Chill. This is about enough custard for a trifle to serve 8.

Line the bottom of a glass serving bowl with sponge-cake slices. Flavor a cup or so of milk with a little sugar and vanilla, and sprinkle enough of this over the cake to moisten it lightly. Spread the cake with the stewed fruit, and chill. When ready to serve, pour the custard sauce over all. You may also decorate the trifle with whipped cream, chopped nuts, and fruit or berries.

GAMES

FOR THIS one the judge has to be on her toes or there will be arguments:

Musical Bumps

Music is played and the children march around the room. When it stops, the last one to sit down is out. Players may sit anywhere—on the sofa, chairs, floor, etc. The music starts again and the game continues until everyone but the last child is out.

Musical Chairs
(*see Game Directory*)

THIS game causes great excitement:

Musical Parcels

The children sit in a circle on the floor. Some small gift has been wrapped in masses of paper and string. The parcel is passed as the music plays. When the music stops, the child holding the parcel tries to unwrap it as much as possible. It must be neatly unwrapped; no tearing of paper allowed and knots must be untied. When the music starts again, he must pass it on and it goes around the circle until the music stops again. The child that gets it unwrapped entirely wins the prize inside.

I have my own variation on this game which I find younger children enjoy. As you wrap the parcel, insert small favors in amongst the paper so that every so often a child uncovers a gift which he may keep. Naturally, make the last favor the best.

Donkey's Tail

Played like Pin the Tail on the Donkey (see Game Directory).

BETTER play this outdoors:

Sardines

One child hides. The other children then have to look for him. When they find him, they stay with him quietly until the last child finally finds them all hiding together. The fun of this is not only the hunt but also the ingenuity of the first child in finding a hiding place where everyone can pack in together and in not getting the giggles and giving away where it is.

For older children:

Question Games

Sheets of paper with questions on some subject appropriate for the age group are given out. The child who answers the most questions correctly wins.

This causes a great deal of excitement and suspense:

Candles

Pennies are arranged on a large dish and each child stands a lit candle on one of them. The first candle to burn away is the winner. The owner of that candle gets all the pennies as a prize.

Better remove valuables, for the room will be turned upside down:

Hunt the Thimble

Everyone must leave the room while a thimble is hidden there. At a signal, the children all come back in and the first to find the thimble is the winner.

FOR junior detectives:

Tray

Several objects are placed on a tray. The tray is shown to all the players for one minute, then it is removed from sight. The players then write down the names of as many of the objects as they can remember. The child that remembers the most wins.

AN EXCITING game for older children. It works out best with at least eight players. (Time was when this was a very popular game with adults, too.)

Murder

A hat is passed containing folded slips of paper, one for each player. One slip says "Detective from Scotland Yard," another says "Murderer," and all the rest say "Witness." *The Murderer must not give away who he is.* Now the Detective leaves the room, and the Murderer identifies himself to the Witnesses.

Then the Detective returns and he stands in one spot from which he may not move, because all the lights in the house are now turned out and the players must know where the Detective is so that he will not be mistaken for anyone else. The Murderer and Witnesses then scatter in the dark throughout the house and keep moving as quietly as possible until the Murderer pounces on someone, who must scream loudly. The Murderer dashes away so that he will be in some unsuspicious spot far from his Victim when the lights are turned back on.

Now everybody goes back to the Detective and he must question the Witnesses to find out who the Murderer was. He can ask all sorts of questions, including where people have been and who they think they bumped into in the dark, but he cannot ask "Who did it?" and he can only ask "Did you do it?" of a Witness once. All the Witnesses must tell the truth, though they may give evasive answers as long as these are not actually untrue. If the Victim is questioned, he must not answer at all, as he is supposed to be dead; the Detective will know that at least this is not the Murderer and the identity of the Victim may give him a clue.

The only person who may lie is the Murderer himself. When the Detective thinks he knows who the Murderer is, he may ask him "Did you do it?" and this is the one question the Murderer must answer truthfully. If the Detective has guessed correctly, he wins a reward. But if he has asked the question of the wrong person, he may not ask any more questions and he is dismissed from Scotland Yard without a reward. The game may be played all over again until a Detective does discover a Murderer and wins the reward.

Prizes are given to game winners at English birthday parties, such as small toys, sweets, or pencils.

In the lower school grades, classmates sing Happy Birthday and give the birthday child "bumps," one for each year and one to grow on. Bumps are given by two people who hold the child under his arms and by the ankles and raise him from the ground and lower him down again for each bump. At home, as a special privilege, the birthday child may stay up later than usual.

On his twenty-first birthday a child comes of age. A large party is given and often "the key to the house" is presented by his father to the birthday celebrant. This is a large silver-colored cardboard key that symbolizes that the owner may now come and go from the house without his parents' permission.

France

SMALL birthday parties are given in France. A few close friends are invited by telephone to come to the house at 4 P.M. for *un goûter* (an afternoon snack). A *goûter* takes place every day at this hour, but on a birthday it is a more elaborate feast and is turned into a party. Since most boys and girls do not attend co-educational schools in France, girls invite only girls to their party and boys have only boys.

Bon Anniversaire, nos voeux les plus sincères (Happy Birthday, our most sincere wishes), the birthday child is greeted. Gifts are placed on his chair and he opens them saying *Merci* (Thank you) to the givers. Toys, books, and accessories are the customary gifts. Clothes are not considered a proper gift for a birthday.

The house is not especially decorated for the party

but the children dress up in their best clothes to attend. Sometimes a costume party is given. The birthday cake is made of any kind of fancy cake, usually with *Bon Anniversaire* written in icing across the top. The same traditions of lighted candles for each year, the secret wish, blowing out the candles, and the first slice of cake for the birthday child are observed. The children sit at table and are served fancily cut sandwiches, chocolates, filled-fruit and hard candies, French pastries, petits-fours, and brioche. Cocoa with whipped cream, or with a crescent-shaped piece of flaky pastry floating on top, and fruit juice are the favorite party drinks. A child of thirteen or older is allowed a glass of champagne with his family as his special birthday treat.

Cat's Tongue Cookies
(Langues de Chat)

9 tablespoons soft sweet butter
10 tablespoons granulated sugar
3 egg whites
1½ cups sifted pastry flour
1½ teaspoons vanilla extract

Preheat oven to 400°F. Work butter and sugar together until smooth and creamy. Add unbeaten egg whites one by one, stirring well after each addition. Resift flour into mixture, add vanilla, and mix again.

Use a pastry tube fitted with a small plain tip. Force 3-inch strips onto a buttered baking sheet, leaving space between each strip. Bake 6 to 8 minutes, or until cookies are lightly browned around the edges. Makes 50–60 pieces.

Charlotte Russe

Lady fingers
1 egg white
¼ cup powdered sugar

1 cup heavy cream, whipped
Vanilla extract

Beat egg white until stiff. Fold in sugar, then fold in whipped cream. Flavor with a few drops of vanilla. Line a glass dessert bowl with lady fingers or thin strips of sponge cake, fill with the whipped mixture, and chill. Serves 4 to 6.

Home movies are often shown at birthday parties in France, or occasionally the birthday child treats his friends to a movie at a local theatre. Games are played at parties, but prizes are not given to game winners.

GAMES

PLAYING house or school is popular at parties for little

girls. Monopoly is always a great favorite, and card games are also played. Other games that are familiar to us in the United States are *Colin-Maillard* (Blindman's Buff), *Câche-câche* (Hide and Seek), *La Tape* (Tag), and Hot Potato. These are all explained in the Game Directory.

As a special privilege, the birthday child may decide the dinner menu and stay up later than usual. The most important birthday, when the child is regarded as an adult, is the eighteenth. And this is the age, too, at which a driving license is obtainable in France.

Germany

THE GERMANS were the first to celebrate children's birthdays, with a party called a *Kinderfeste* (children's festival), but today they call it a birthday party (*Geburtstag Fest*).

Alles gute zum Geburtstag (Everything good for your birthday, or Happy Birthday) the child is greeted when he awakens. His chair at the breakfast table is laden with gifts from his family. It is customary to open them before starting breakfast, and the child says *Danke* (Thank you) to each gift giver. Toys, books, and clothes are usual birthday gifts although occasionally a relative gives money as a present. The family joins him as he reads his birthday cards which have an appropriate picture and verse on them.

Party invitations are not sent out, as guests are

invited in person to German birthday parties. Usually the celebration is at home, though sometimes the children are taken out for a special treat such as a marionette show. Flowers, balloons, and streamers decorate the house, and "slingers" are hung on the walls. Slingers are elaborately cut tissue-paper designs that, when opened up, form three-dimensional figures of flowers, leaves, dolls, animals, etc. Some slingers open up into a crescent moon with a tissue-paper birthday candle in the middle. The table is set with linen and with china dishes, but paper napkins with a birthday picture and greeting printed on them are used. There is a party hat at each place.

The birthday cake is a layer cake frosted with butter cream, chocolate frosting, or whipped cream and decorated with marzipan flowers. Very often a seven-layer cake is used. Sometimes small charms are baked into the cake and the children who find them in their slices of cake keep the charms. Happy Birthday to —————(name)—————, or For the —————(years)————— Birthday, is written across the top of the cake. Candles, called the "Light of Life," are set in a circle around the edge, and there is an extra candle to grow on besides one for each year for the birthday child to blow out after making his secret wish. The first slice is served to him. Besides the birthday cake, candy (nougat, marzipan, or nuts coated with chocolate), and cocoa with whipped cream are served.

The best-known German birthday song is different from ours:

Ich freue mich dass ich geboren bin	I am happy that I was born
Und habe Geburtstag heute.	And celebrate my birthday today.
Man hat mich lieb	They love me so
Und schenkt mir viel:	And give me so much:
Zum essen, putzen und zum spiel.	To eat, to wear and games to play.
Ich freue mich dass ich geboren bin	I am happy that I was born
Und habe Geburtstag heute.	And celebrate my birthday today.

Seven-Layer Cake

6 eggs, separated
1¼ cups sugar
2 tablespoons lemon juice
⅔ cup sifted flour
¼ cup cornstarch
½ teaspoon salt
Creamy Chocolate Frosting (next page)

With a rotary beater, beat egg yolks until thick and lemon colored. Add sugar gradually, still beating constantly, and add 1 tablespoon of the lemon juice. Sift together flour, cornstarch, and salt, and add this bit by bit, alternating with drops of the remaining tablespoon of lemon juice. Beat batter until it is smooth. Then beat egg whites until stiff, and fold these into batter.

Line two or three shallow (1 inch deep) 8-inch layer

pans with paper, and grease lightly. Spread a few spoonfuls of batter in each pan, and bake in a 450°F. (very hot) oven for 5 minutes, or until lightly browned. Remove and let cool. Repeat baking process until all batter is used and seven layers are baked. Peel off all scraps of paper lining. Stack the layers one on top of the other, with Creamy Chocolate Frosting between all the layers, and cover top and sides of the cake with more frosting.

Creamy Chocolate Frosting

¾ cup sugar
¾ cup heavy cream
1¼ cups shaved chocolate (4 ounces German's sweet chocolate and 3 ounces unsweetened chocolate)

Mix together sugar and cream. Cook over low heat just until mixture boils. Place shaved chocolate in a bowl, and pour hot cream over it slowly. Beat until chocolate melts and makes a smooth frosting. Add a little cream if it is too thick for spreading.

German Punch

1 cup grape juice
1 cup cider
½ cup grapefruit juice
1 quart soda water
Sugar to taste

Mix and pour over a large cake of ice in a punch bowl.

SOME GERMAN children receive when they are christened a large candle with twelve or so markings spaced out on it from top to bottom. Each year at birthdaytime, the candle is burned down to the next marking.

Twelve-Year Candle

1¼ pounds paraffin
1¼ pounds beeswax
Colored wax crayons
  1 yard soft white string
  1 teaspoon salt
  2 teaspoons borax
  ⅓ cup water
A little melted candle wax or beeswax

Small piece of cardboard
Tape (masking or any adhesive tape)
1-quart mold (mailing tube for round candle, or milk carton with ends cut off for square candle)
Small block of ice

The parafin has a low melting point, so drips freely. The beeswax hardens the candle. All beeswax (2½ pounds) may be used if you wish. This amount will fill a 1-quart mold. Hobby and crafts shops carry candle-making supplies, or see the Mail Order Shopping Directory.

To make wick: Do this a day or two before making the candle. Dissolve salt and borax in water, and soak string in this for about 2 hours. Take out string and let dry. The salt and borax keep the string from burning too rapidly and from fizzing out.

Cut string 2 inches or more longer than needed to make a wick the length of the mold. Melt a little wax in a double boiler and dip wick into it. Take wick out to let wax drip down, and dip again. Hang wick up to dry; *it must hang straight.* When wax has stiffened the string and is completely dry, the wick is ready to use.

To make candle: Place wick before pouring wax. Cut a circle or square of cardboard that will cover the end of the mold you are using, and punch a hole in the center. Make a knot in one end of the wick, and pull wick through the hole; the knot will anchor it. Tape the cardboard to one end of the mailing tube, with the wick hanging down inside.

Melt the paraffin and beeswax in the top of a double boiler. Don't get it smoking hot. To color, with a knife shave a colored wax crayon into the melted wax. One crayon is enough to color this amount. Or use two crayons for dark shades, three for black or white. Use one quarter to one half crayon for pastels. Stir well to blend.

Stand mold on a piece of ice when you pour the hot wax into it so that it will harden immediately and not run out. Pull the wick straight through the tube or carton and hold it steady in the center as you pour the wax. After the wax has hardened, peel the tube or carton off. Rub a soft cloth with wax, and use this to rub the candle gently to polish it.

To decorate candle: Candle can be marked with twelve lines and the numbers of twelve years with colored magic marker. Designs can also be drawn on candle and decorated with sequins, glitter, metallic braid and tape, artificial flowers leaves, ornaments, butterflies, small charms, colored stars, small bells, etc.

To sprinkle with glitter, redip finished candle into a bath of melted wax the same color. Drain briefly, but don't allow to harden. Sprinkle with glitter and then let dry completely.

Other decorations are stuck to the candle with drops of melted wax the same color, though some can be stuck right into the candle. To put sequins on, for instance, cut straight pins short with a wire cutter, and push pins through the holes in the sequins into the candle. Artificial flowers with wire stems cut short can be pushed into the candle the same way (add a little melted wax if needed to hold flowers steady).

Name candle: Spell out name and birthday greeting with silver or gold letters that come in paper sheets, easy to punch out. Stick letters on the candle with melted wax.

Special charm candle: Another idea is to decorate a candle entirely with good-luck charms—a horseshoe for luck, coin for wealth, ring for marriage, bluebird for happiness, etc. Each charm may be ringed with glitter, sequins, or stars.

GAMES

SMALL GIRLS and boys love this one. It is simply a version of London Bridge, which is played in so many countries around the world (see Game Directory).

Golden Bridge

Two children hold hands and make a bridge. Each secretly decides what he will represent (historic character, moon, sun, whatever). The other children form a line and march under the bridge chanting:

> *Golden bridge, golden bridge,*
> *Golden bridge over the water,*
> *Who broke you?*
> *The goldsmith and his daughter.*
> *All march through,*
> *All march through,*
> *With spear and rod held over you.*

The bridge is lowered when the song ends, and a child is caught. The two bridge children secretly whisper what they represent to the caught child. He decides which one he will join and goes to stand behind his choice. The game is repeated until all the children have chosen a side. A Tug-of-War decides the winning side.

AN OLD favorite, very like Simon Says (see Game Directory):

Adam Had Seven Sons

All stand in a circle with IT in the middle and chant:

> *Adam had seven sons,*
> *Seven sons had Adam.*
> *They ate not,*
> *They drank not.*
> *All do as I do,*
> *As I do.*

As they chant "as I do," the child that is IT does something and all do as he does (flap his arms, scratch his foot, make a face, jump, etc.)

A GREAT game for boys:

Dog Collar

For two players or two teams of players evenly divided into pairs. Two players, on all fours, face each other. Both their heads are in a loop of strong cloth; a belt can be used for the loop. A line or marker separates the two players. At the signal of "Go!", opponents try to pull each other across the line separating them. At the end of one minute, the winner is the one who at that moment has gotten his opponent pulled over to his own side of the line.

Blinde Kuh

This is Blindman's Buff (see Game Directory).

Reise Nach Jerusalem
(Journey to Jerusalem)

This is the game of Musical Chairs (see Game Directory).

Hali-Halo

The player who is IT holds a ball. He gives hints as to what thing or place he is thinking about. (For example: It's a city in Germany starting with M.) When the answer is guessed correctly, he drops the ball and the winning guesser runs for it and throws the ball at IT. If he hits him, he gets the chance to be IT.

Kommando Bimberle

Everyone sits around a table. One child commands: "Do this with your hands," or "*Don't* do this with your hands." If a child does the wrong thing, he must put something that belongs to him on the table. When a previously specified number of objects are on the table, the children to whom they belong must redeem them by doing whatever forfeit stunts they are told (see page 187).

THIS GAME is one of our favorites. It is better played with not too large a group. If you have a camera, use it; the goings-on are hilarious:

Chocolate Bar

The game requires a hat, scarf, gloves, knife and fork, a wrapped bar of chocolate, and dice. The children take turns throwing the dice. When one gets a double, he quickly puts on the hat, scarf, and gloves, and tries to undo the chocolate bar with the knife and fork and then to eat as much of it as he can, still using only the knife and fork. Meanwhile the children go on throwing the dice. The child working on the chocolate bar may continue until someone else throws a double. Then that child quickly puts on the hat, scarf, and gloves, and tries his luck at the chocolate bar.

Prizes of small toys or candy are given to children who win the games. Hans Christian Andersen stories and Grimm's fairy tales are sometimes told to children at birthday parties, too.

The most important birthday in Germany is the twenty-first and signifies being grown-up and independent. The privileges of the birthday child are the familiar ones—he is given his favorite foods, he is excused from his regular chores, he may stay up later than usual, and, a special custom in Germany, his place at table is decorated with flowers.

Holland

IN HOLLAND, birthdays are divided into odd years, called half Crown years, and even years, called Crown years. If you are celebrating a Crown year, you receive larger and more expensive gifts and have a more elaborate party than you could hope for on a half Crown year. Before his birthday draws near, the birthday child makes a *Verlanglijst*, which is a list of the gifts that he would like to receive. The list is available to anyone who wants to give a present. As the donor of a gift decides what he will give, he makes a cross next to it on the list to show that it will be taken care of.

Early on the morning of the birthday, while the birthday child is still asleep, his parents and brothers and sisters gather together to decorate his chair at the dining table. If it is summertime, they hang garlands of flowers from the chair. In winter, evergreens, streamers, and colorful bows are used. The family greets the birthday child with *Hartelijk Gefeliciteerd Met Je Verjaardag* (Hearty congratulations for your birthday), and then they sing:

Lang zal hij leven,	Long may he live,
Lang zal hij leven,	Long may he live,
Lang zal hij leven,	Long may he live,
In de gloria,	In prosperity,
Hiep, hiep, hoera!	Hip, hip, hurrah!

The house is decorated with balloons, streamers, ribbons and bows, and lots of flowers in vases everywhere. Slingers like those used in Germany (page 63) are hung from the walls and placed on the table. Party invitations are not sent out but family, friends, and neighbors remember the date and arrive to celebrate the birthday. There is open house all day.

Guests are greeted with a cheery *Daag* (Hello), and *Dank U Wel* (Thank you) is said to each gift giver. Birthday cards are sent only if it is impossible to attend the open house and give good wishes in person. Birthday cards in Holland are single cards like postcards and a birthday picture and greeting are printed on the front.

The table is set with candles and good linen and china and is laden with *Taartjes* that are served all day to the visitors. *Taartjes* are small, very fancy pastries covered with sweet icing or whipped cream and with rich fillings or fruits inside, very much like some French pastries. Candies are not often offered, though sometimes Dutch chocolates are. A large birthday cake may be served some time during the day as a dessert. It may have candles on it, one for each year, and if there are candles the birthday child blows them out, but the secret wish is not traditional. Coffee and tea are served to adults and the children drink lemonade.

Taartjes

2 cups sifted flour	⅔ cup shortening
1 teaspoon salt	4 tablespoons water

Mix ingredients and handle as for any pie dough. Fit pastry over the backs of little individual pie pans or fluted tart pans, and prick all over to prevent puffing. Bake in a 475°F. (very hot) oven for 8 to 10 minutes. Cool. Makes twelve tarts each about 3½ inches in diameter.

If you make *Taartjes* in quantity for a big party, use a variety of fillings—fruit, custard, chocolate cream, etc., and, depending on the filling, top with meringue, whipped cream, nuts, cherries, sliced fruit glazed with melted fruit jam or jelly, or prebaked pastry cut-outs.

Pleated Slingers

Cut a piece of colored paper or tissue paper about 3

inches wide and 20 inches long. Accordion-pleat the paper, making each fold about 1 inch wide. When the paper is all folded, starting at one side and about ¼ inch from the top, draw the outline of half of a small figure or flower on the top fold. The outline should not come too near the opposite side and should end about ¼ inch from the bottom of the side on which it began. Cut around the outline with scissors, cutting through all the folds at the same time. Unfold and attach a string to either end for hanging as a decoration.

Candlestick Ornaments

Cover the top of plastic candle coasters *(bobêches)* with glue, and mold a thin layer of clay over it. Glue ornaments (tiny pine cones, acorns, berries, colored beads, tiny Christmas balls, etc.) to the clay. Cover the entire surface, but leave the center candle hole free. When glue is dry, spray decorations with varnish or clear lacquer.

GAMES

Groene Zwanen, Witte Zwanen
(Green Swan, White Swan)

This is the Dutch London Bridge (see Game Directory).

Zakdoekje Leggen

The same as Drop the Handkerchief (see Game Directory).

Stoelendans

Played like Musical Chairs (see Game Directory).

Ezeltje Prikken

Pin the Tail on the Donkey (see Game Directory).

No prizes are given for winning games, nor are special party favors given to the guests, except for the balloons, which are given to the children when they go home.

The birthday child brings hard candies such as *Hopjes* to school to treat his classmates, and they sing the birthday song in his honor. The special privileges for the birthday child are again familiar ones—choosing the dinner menu for the family and staying up later than usual.

Iceland

SPECIAL occasions such as birthdays call for a treat such as a dish of canned fruit which is a great rarity in Iceland. All families in Iceland celebrate birthdays, but the house is not especially decorated for the party. It is not the custom to give party favors nor prizes for winning games. The Icelandic child is greeted with *Til Hamingju Med Afmaelisdaginn* (To happiness with your birthday).

The birthday child greets his guests with *Hallo* (Hello, as said to a child), *Komdu Saell* (Come with health, as said to a man), and *Komdu Sael* (Come with health, as said to a woman). The usual presents of money, or a book, given by a friend are received with *Pakka pér Tyrir* (formal Thank you) or *Takk* (informal Thank you).

The birthday cake is round and thickly covered with whipped cream and, in this country, too, the birthday child receives the first slice. Canned fruit slices are sometimes put on the top, or occasionally canned fruit is served, perhaps with whipped cream on it, as a special birthday dessert. There are no candles on the cake, and there is no special Icelandic birthday song. In the evening, the birthday child will have the familiar privilege of being allowed to stay up later than usual.

Pönnukökur are always served at the birthday party. These are paper-thin round pancakes that are spread with strawberry preserves and whipped cream. They are served folded in wedge shapes. No other food is customarily served at the party except for chocolate candy and hot cocoa with whipped cream.

Pönnukökur

1¼ cups flour
½ teaspoon salt
½ teaspoon baking powder
2 cups milk
1 egg

Butter or shortening for skillet
Sugar
Jam
Whipped cream

Sift flour, salt, and baking powder together. Stir in milk gradually. Beat eggs lightly and add to dry ingredients, stirring everything well together.

Heat a small (9-inch) very shallow griddle-like iron

skillet. Keep heat medium to low and grease griddle lightly. Pour a small amount of the mixture into the pan so that when it is tilted the batter will cover the bottom; the pancakes should be paper thin. Bake till light brown on the bottom, then turn and do the other side. This should take about a minute or less. Grease the griddle whenever necessary while making the *pönnukökur*, but only slightly.

After making each pancake, sprinkle it with a little sugar on the side that was baked last. This will keep them soft. Serve warm or cold, in either of two ways:

Spread a spoonful of your favorite jam on each pancake, on the side that was baked last, and either roll up or fold to look like a wedge of pie.

Spread jam as above, and on top put a spoonful of whipped cream, but don't spread this. Then fold over as before.

GAMES

ALWAYS a favorite and known in many countries. In Iceland it is called *Fela Hlutinn*.

Hide the Object, or Hot and Cold

One child hides some object while the other children are out of the room. When the others return, they hunt for it and the child who hid the object tells them if they are HOT (coming near the hidden item) or COLD (moving away from it) as they hunt.

A GOOD indoor or outdoor game for young children:

Inn Og Ut Um Gluggan
(In and Out the Window)

The children form a circle, holding hands in a raised position. One child stands in the middle. When music begins, the child weaves in and out between the children in the circle, under their upraised arms. When the song stops, the child stops in front of the nearest child in the circle. That child then grabs the first child's waist and, when the music starts again, they both weave in tandem around the circle. The game goes on until no one is left in the circle.

Spin the Bottle

The children stand in a circle and a bottle is spun in the center. The child the bottle points to when it comes to rest must do a stunt or pay a forfeit (see page 187).

ANOTHER popular forfeit game at Icelandic birthday parties is also played in Denmark; see *Pantelege,* page 46.

IN THE following Icelandic game, everyone stands in a circle. One child sits in the center on the floor and recites:

> Alone I sit and sew.
> Nobody comes to see me but the little mouse.

Then the child jumps up and says:

> I point East.
> I point West.

The child then closes his eyes and turns round and round. He finally stops and points his finger toward the circle, and then opens his eyes. The child he is pointing to becomes the next one in the center.

THE GAME we know as London Bridge (see Game Directory) is also played in Iceland. The two children who make the bridge usually choose for the secret characters they represent one of the personages of the Icelandic sagas. These sagas are folktales and legends based on the history of the country and the characters are historical figures. They are often told to children at parties. One of the well-known Icelandic sagas is called . . .

WHY HARALD WOULD NOT CUT HIS HAIR

LONG AGO, in the days when Norway was divided into

many small warring kingdoms, Prince Harald was ruler of a little district in the southern part of the country.

One day while traveling, Harald came upon a very beautiful girl. When he inquired about her, he discovered that she was Gyda, the daughter of a wealthy chieftain. Prince Harald made further inquiries about her and arranged to meet her. He found her to be intelligent and charming, and he realized that he was in love with her. Harald was determined to marry her. But when he sent messengers to propose the marriage, Gyda told them that she would not marry a ruler of such a small district. She promised to marry Prince Harald only when he had united all of Norway under his rule.

Instead of being angry and forcing the marriage, the Prince thought over her message. He decided to fulfill her request and made a vow not to cut or comb his hair until Norway was united under his hand.

As it happened, a short time thereafter some neighboring chieftains decided to invade Harald's lands. They attacked in full force but, since Harald had been a wise and just ruler, his subjects rose up to fight the invaders. Harald routed the enemy and followed them to their own countries and occupied their lands. Because he was just and good, the conquered people liked him and came willingly under his rule. More and more people of influence came to join Harald and joined forces with him, and he became more and more powerful. But some jealous and warlike neighbors feared his power and tried to hatch plots and intrigues against the fair-haired Harald. Finally all the kings outside Harald's kingdom banded together to fight him.

The fighting at Hafs Fiord was long and bitter and bloody, but Harald and his people were resolved to win and they fought magnificently. At long last, the battle was over and Harald was victor. He was now King of all Norway. For the first time in history Norway was a united land. But those people who still did not want to submit to Harald's laws were allowed to leave the country. They gathered together with their families and household goods and decided to go to a little-known island out in the sea where there was a wilderness of mountains, treeless plains, and glaciers. It resembled Norway somewhat, but was unsettled. So the defeated chiefs decided to make this island, called Iceland, their new home and they sailed off. When they approached the island, they threw an object overboard into the ocean. They agreed to build their new settlement at the spot where it was washed ashore. They named this place Smoky Bay and today it is the capital of Iceland and is called Reykjavik.

Harald celebrated his victory with a banquet at which he had his hair cut and combed. His was so handsome that the lords at the dinner acclaimed him Harald Fair-Hair, by which name he was thereafter known. Harald now sent word to Gyda of his victory and bade her fulfill her promise, which she was more than happy to do.

And so this is why it is said that it was Gyda who brought about the unification of Norway and caused Iceland to be settled.

Ireland

An Irish child is given "bumps" on his birthday, as is done in England. His friends lift him by the ankles and under the arms and they bump him on the ground once for each year and once more for luck. Birthday cards from family and friends greet the birthday child on the day of his celebration. His school chums often make their own special cards to send him.

Birthday invitations, or personal letters, have been sent out to friends and relatives in advance of the party day. Ordinarily, the party is held at home, though occasionally the birthday child will treat his friends to a movie or a pantomime. Colored balloons decorate the house festively. The birthday table is set with a paper table cloth with birthday decorations and greetings printed on it. Party favors are placed next to the colorful paper plates and napkins at each child's setting. Different small toys (marbles, small car or doll, etc.) are used as party favors.

Popsickle Doll

Popsickle sticks   Crayons or paints
Milk-bottle caps   Wool
Glue or stapler   Colored paper
Heavy thread   Clay

Glue or staple milk cap to end of one stick. Cut two sticks in half to make arms and legs, and make holes in ends of each. Make two holes in stick body and fasten on arms and legs with thread and knot. Draw or paint face on milk cap. Glue on strands of wool for hair. Cut out dress or suit from paper and glue to stick body, front and back. Make little clay mounds for feet and stick legs into them so that doll will stand.

Spool Doll

Spools of different sizes   Colored yarn
Beads   Crayons or paints
Buttons

String together different sized spools to make body, arms, legs, and head of doll, using buttons and beads to hold yarn at ends. The various extremities can all have their strings pass through a big center spool used for the body and up through a head spool if you are clever about it, so that one big woolly knot that serves for hair holds the doll together. Crayon or paint a face on the head spool.

Candy Creatures

Marshmallows	Toothpicks
Gumdrops	Licorice stick

Make body and head of an imaginary animal with marshmallows put together with toothpicks. Make ears of gumdrops cut in half, and make legs of several gumdrops strung on toothpicks. Use toothpicks to put all parts together, and stick in bits of licorice stick for eyes.

Irish birthday parties are similar to the English custom of high tea. Little sandwiches, cookies, and candy are offered when the guests sit down at the table. Various types of candies served are toffees, chocolates with filled centers, jelly slices, and hard sugar candies. The birthday cake is a round fruit cake frosted with a white, hard sugar icing. Flowers made of colored hard sugar icing decorate it. Happy Birthday to ——(name)—— is written across the top, usually in pink or blue icing. There are candles on the cake, one for each year, and the birthday child makes his secret wish and blows them out before he is given the first piece.

A specialty of birthday parties in Ireland is the trifle, which is made differently from the English trifle. It is a special type of cake, served as a dessert. A layer of plain custard is poured into a large bowl, then pieces of sponge cake are cut into the custard before it thickens. After it thickens, a layer of flavored custard is added and that is allowed to set. This process is repeated for as many layers as desired. The top is finished off with a layer of the flavored custard and sprinkled with oblong crystals of colored sugar called Hundreds and Thousands. Lemonade and Coke are the popular party drinks.

Fruit Cake

1 cup soft shortening	1 teaspoon salt
2 cups brown sugar	1 cup liquid (jelly, mo-
4 large eggs	lasses, coffee, etc.)
3 cups sifted flour	Candied fruits
1 teaspoon baking pow-	Chopped nuts
der	

Cream together shortening and sugar until fluffy. Beat in eggs. Sift together the flour, baking powder, and salt, and stir gradually into egg mixture, alternating with portions of the cup of liquid. Blend in the candied fruits and nuts.

Line two 9" x 5" x 3" loaf pans with heavy wrapping paper, and grease. Fill pans almost full, and bake fruit cakes in 300°F. (slow) over for 2½ to 3 hours, until a toothpick stuck in comes out clean. Cover with greased paper for the last hour. Cool, and store wrapped in waxed paper or foil.

The Irish birthday song is the same as the one sung in the United States. During the party, family and friends present their gifts, which are usually toys and clothes, although occasionally relatives give money to put into the child's savings account.

GAMES

THIS WILL set the girls giggling:

Squeak Piggy Squeak

The children sit in a circle. One child is IT and stands in the center of the circle. He is blindfolded and he holds a pillow. He walks around the circle and then places his pillow on someone's lap. He sits down on it and says, "Squeak Piggy Squeak." The child that he is sitting on must make noises. The blindfolded child must try to guess whom he is sitting on by the sounds that he has heard. If he guesses correctly, then the child he was sitting on becomes IT.

GREAT FUN and excitement:

Pass the Orange

Two teams are set up. The first child in each team places an orange under his chin and puts his hands behind his back. At a signal, the first child in each team must pass the orange from under his chin to the next member of his team, who must receive it under his chin. No hands may be used. The orange is passed back through the entire team. If the orange is dropped, the team must start all over again. The first team that successfully passes the orange through its ranks wins.

Pass the Parcel

They all love this—especially the winner! See Musical Parcels, page 53.

Blindman's Buff
(see Game Directory)

Pin the Tail on the Donkey
(see Game Directory)

Hide and Seek
(see Game Directory)

Musical Chairs
(see Game Directory)

Forfeit Games
(*see* Pantelege, *page 46*)

AN EXCITING card game:

Snap

Two or more can play. A deck of cards is dealt out, and the hands are held stacked and face down. The children then all turn up one card from their hands. If any child spots a card of the same number as his, he calls SNAP. The first child to call gets all the turned up cards. Or, if there are no doubles to call, the next cards are turned up, and so on. The winner is the child who gets all his opponent's cards if only two children are playing. If more than two players are involved, the winner is the one with the most cards when one player runs out of cards.

Small gifts are given as prizes to game winners (toy cars, inexpensive books, skipping ropes, etc.). The children often do the Irish Step Dance at parties and enjoy singing together. Songs like "Danny Boy," "The Minstrel Boy," and "Irish Lullaby" are old favorites. Stories told about leprechauns or banshees are greatly enjoyed by Irish children.

The class sings Happy Birthday to the birthday child at school, and the teacher often gives him candy as a treat in his honor. He is allowed to stay up later than usual and—if possible!—he is given his own way all day.

The twenty-first birthday signifies coming of age. A large party is usually given and is often held in a hired hall. A cardboard key to the house is presented to the birthday celebrant by his parents, as is done in England. It is elaborately wrapped and a great ceremony is made over the giving of it. Greeting cards for this birthday have a picture of the key on them and very often a black cat sits on the key. The black cat is considered lucky.

Israel

IN THE CITIES

ALL CLASSMATES are always invited to every birthday party in Israel. As a result, birthday parties are big events, with thirty or more children attending. The birthday child is greeted with *Yom Holedet Sameach* (Happy Birthday) by his teacher in school and his classmates. The teacher announces the birthday in class and tells the children what day the party will be held.

Most parties are held at home, which is usually in an apartment house. The family of the birthday child empties the largest room of all furniture except the serving table and one decorated chair that the birthday child will sit on. They deck the house with balloons and occasionally use streamers, and they are ready for guests early, knowing that in Israel it is the custom for children to arrive an hour earlier than the invitation called for. The children do not dress up for a birthday party.

Dishes of fruit slices, nuts, raisins, small iced cup-cakes, or slices of plain sponge cake, and a dish of hard candy are on the table. Fruit juice is the favored birth-day-party drink. The children are served buffet style, and they sit on the floor and play some of the party games while eating. Plates are not used, as everything served can be held in the hands. Decorative party nap-kins are provided almost as a favor rather than for use because many children in Israel make a hobby of col-lecting them. A birthday cake with candles is seldom used, nor is a birthday wish made.

Taiglach
(Israeli Honey Clusters)

¾ cup flour	½ cup honey
1 egg	¼ teaspoon powdered
½ teaspoon salt	ginger

Sift the flour. Stir the egg, then mix together flour, egg, and salt. Knead the dough, adding flour if it is too sticky. Divide it in half, roll each section into a rope ⅓ of an inch thick. Cut these into ½-inch pieces, and place them on a well-greased baking sheet. Bake in a

375°F. oven for 15 minutes, until golden brown, turning the pieces once with a spatula to brown them on both sides.

Now boil the honey with the ginger in a saucepan. Add the baked *taiglach* and boil gently for 20 minutes, stirring with a wooden spoon. Pour out onto a lightly greased plate, and separate the pieces. Let cool.

The birthday child greets his friends with *Shalom* (Hello), and if they give him a gift he says *Todah* (Thank you). The giving of birthday presents is not considered necessary in Israel. Getting together with friends to celebrate and have fun is the most important and exciting part of a birthday. Friends sometimes do bring small things such as a candy bar or a homemade gift, or make a picture scrapbook to give as a present. Gifts are *never* opened while guests are still in the house.

Pencil Holder

Juice or soup can with lid taken off	Paper of several colors Glue

Cover can all over with small cut-out designs. They may be glued on to cover the whole surface by overlapping the cutouts, or a solid piece of colored paper may be glued to the can first and designs added afterwards.

Picture **Plate**

Large paper plate   Ribbon
Crayons or paints   Scotch tape
Shellac and shellac brush

Draw a picture on the center of the plate, color the picture, then color a decorative design around the edge. Shellac the plate. Make a loop of ribbon and tape it to the back of the plate so that the picture can be hung.

At some time during the party the children sing the birthday song:

> *Yom Holedet, Yom Holedet, Chagigah hayom,*
> *Chaverim v'chaverot gshu na gshu halum.*
> L ——(name)—— *chavertenu mal'u* ——(number)——
> *shanim.*
> *Sov' vuah v'yitnu lah kabalat panim*
> *Al kisei ram noshiveah*
> *Zer prachim n'atreah*
> *'Mala 'mala narimeah*
> *Zen yizcheh l'shanah tova.*

This is translated:

> Birthday, birthday, today is a festival,
> Friends, boys and girls, please come closer.
> ——(name)—— is now ——(number)—— years
> old.

Turn him around and give him a warm welcome.
Seat him on a throne,
Crown him with a wreath of flowers
Raise him up high and even higher
May he have a good year.

During the singing, the birthday child is seated on the special chair that has been decorated for him with flowers or greens. At the point in the song where it says to crown him with a wreath, the children put a wreath of flowers on his head. And when the song says to raise him up, the children lift him, chair and all, once for each year and one more time to grow on.

Flower Headband

Strip of felt about 24 inches by 2 inches
2 snaps
Felt scraps in gay colors, or artificial flowers
Needle and thread, or glue

Sew snaps on ends of band so it will fit at the correct head size. Cut flower petals and leaves from colored felt and sew or glue onto band, covering the middle 8 inches of it. Or decorate by sewing on artificial flowers.

All during the party, the children sing various popular songs or folk songs. Circle dancing is extremely popular, and the children often tell funny stories to one another, too.

GAMES

A GAME of skill:

Peanuts in the Bottle

A bottle is placed on the floor. A child kneels on a chair, with one hand behind his back. With the other hand he tries to drop peanuts into the bottle.

Jacks and Ball
(see Game Directory)

Blindman's Buff
(see Game Directory)

Name Games

Such as, name as many flowers as possible, or trees, or famous men in various categories, etc.

Musical Chairs
(see Game Directory)

Red Light
(see Game Directory)

Hide and Seek

This is not the Hide and Seek we usually think of by that name, but the HOT and COLD game known in many countries and called Hide the Object in its Icelandic version described on page 80. In this Israeli version, the group of children *sing* as one child looks for an object they have hidden, and they sing softly when he is far from it and louder and louder as he comes near it.

Some games require a forfeit being paid. A favorite one is to tie a carrot by a string around the waist of the child. It dangles to the rear and a lit candle is placed on the floor. The candle must be put out with the carrot by having the child squat down to extinguish the flame.

I can just picture the faces of many mothers after reading this. But, if carefully supervised, it isn't as dangerous as it sounds. The children are thrilled by the excitement, and a handy bucket of water should calm even the nervous.

Small prizes (crayons, an inexpensive toy, cards, etc.) are given to winners of the games. Favors of ballons, a bag of candy and cake, crayons, or some other small item are given to the guests when they go home.

The thirteenth birthday is the most important one

for an Israeli boy. This is the age of Bar Mitzvah, when a boy is considered to have become a man. The boy accepts the Torah and promises to live up to its laws. The Torah is the scroll of Hebrew Law. The Bar Mitzvah is celebrated on the Saturday nearest to the thirteenth birthday. The boy wears new clothes for the occasion and goes to the synagogue with his parents. He takes his place at the altar and repeats a section of the scroll of the Torah. He gives a short talk before the congregation explaining what the Bar Mitzvah ceremony means to him. He discusses the chapter that he has read from the Torah and thanks his parents, family, and friends for all they have done for him during his thirteen years. After the ceremony he returns home, usually to a party given by his parents in his honor. Often a dinner is served and family and friends are invited to join the celebration. In honor of his Bar Mitzvah, the boy receives gifts of books, pens, wallets, clothes, money, and any item that the gift giver feels he would enjoy having.

ON THE KIBBUTZ

KIBBUTZ life is different from life in the cities. Almost everything is owned by the community rather than by the individual. The children usually live with their classmates at the school, rather than with their parents. The parents visit their children after they have completed their day's work or whenever they have leisure time.

The community provides the refreshments for a child's birthday party, which is held in the classroom, or outdoors if the weather permits. Everyone dresses up for the party. All the classmates of the birthday child and his family and relatives are invited to the celebration, which the child's mother and his teacher conduct together. Birthdays are often celebrated on the Friday nearest to the actual birth date, so that relatives from other areas can attend.

If the party is held indoors, the room is decorated with balloons, streamers, and flowers. The birthday child sits on his special chair which is decorated with flowers and greens, and when the birthday song is sung the children lift him in it and crown him with a wreath of flowers just as the city children do. No special birthday cake is customary, but an iced layer cake is served and the birthday child is presented with the first slice. But there are no candles on the cake, and no wish is made. Hard candies, fruit slices, and a fruit drink or hot cocoa are served to the guests at the party table.

The children do a lot of singing on the Kibbutzim, with children's songs and folk songs being the most popular at birthday parties. Circle dances are done frequently, too.

GAMES

GAMES AND entertainment at a Kibbutz birthday party differ somewhat from those enjoyed in the cities.

Hail, O King

A child is chosen as King. He sits on a throne. The other children decide in secret on a story that they can act out in pantomine. Parts are assigned and they return to the King.

> *They say:* Hail, O King.
> *King:* Where have you been?
> *They:* Far away in the forest.
> *King:* And what have you been doing?

The group then acts out its pantomine, and the King must guess what the story is about.

VERY exciting—and not too easy:

Bli Yadayim
(Without Hands)

Players are divided into groups of four or five players. Each group stands in a row and the players have a rope in front of them which they all hold onto with both hands. A short distance away from each group, a hat for each player on the team is placed on the ground. At the signal, the teams rush forward, still holding their ropes, and try to get the hats on their heads without using hands. Players can help each other by using head, teeth, or feet. If a player lets go of the rope or uses his hands, the team is disqualified. The first team to return to its starting place wearing all its hats wins.

BETTER played outdoors:

Ben Hur

This is relay race. Two brooms are needed. Two teams are formed. Two people from each team enter the "arena." They are Ben Hur and his horse, the broom is the carriage. Ben Hur sits on the broom bristles, facing the horse and hanging onto the broom handle. He is dragged by the horse, who pulls the broom by the handle. At the signal, the carriages race to the goal and back to the starting point. The winners of each relay get a point for their team. The team with the most points at the finish of the game wins.

Musical Chairs
(see Game Directory)

Relay Races

Continuous relay races are familiar in many countries; for example, the old-fashioned potato (or hard-boiled-egg) race called *Stafetlø* in Denmark (see page 47) or the Sack Race (see Game Directory).

There are no prizes for game winners, but favors, such as bag of hard candies, raisins, nuts, or a piece of cake, and balloons are given to the guests when the party is over. Puppet shows and shadow plays put on by the children or by adults are birthday-party treats in Israel. The children love to hear fairy tales or hero stories, and the well-known "Dr. Doolittle" stories have become great favorites with them.

At some Kibbutzim, the guests voluntarily give a contribution to the Jewish National Fund in honor of the birthday child. Guests do not usually bring gifts to the birthday child, though sometimes a few children will make something for him. Often the teacher gives him a present. A book is her customary choice, though sometimes she will give a set of paints or some other small token. The parents of the child give him a present, and they usually give a gift to the school in honor of his birthday, such as a set of homemade blocks, homemade toys, or playground equipment that they have constructed themselves.

The special privilege of the Israeli birthday child is to go home on the night of his birthday to sleep in his parents' room at the Kibbutz.

Italy

BEFORE World War II, children in Italy celebrated
their Saint's Name Day instead of their own birth
dates. Very often an Italian child's birthday falls on
his Saint's Name Day, but many times it may not.
Nowadays, the child's actual birthday is celebrated,
though many families celebrate both events.

The house is not especially decorated for a birthday
party, but it is often filled with flowers because the
giving of flowers by friends and relatives to someone
celebrating a birthday is an old Italian custom.

Paper Flowers

Sheets of differently colored tissue paper
Green pipe cleaners or florist's wire

Tear strips of colored tissue paper about 4 inches long. Roll strips loosely to form flowers. Uneven, torn edges provide a natural petal look. Twist the bottom end of the flower and curl a piece of pipe cleaner or wire around the flower bottom to make a stem and hold the flower together. For a more varied flower, roll two differently colored strips of tissue paper together to form the flower. Bouquets of tissue-paper flowers are gay decorations for a party table.

The birthday child invites friends to his home to help him celebrate. Everyone dresses in his best clothes for the occasion. Friends greet the birthday child with *Buon Campleanno* (Happy Birthday), and he says *Grazie* (Thank you) as they give him their gifts. Clothing and money are the customary birthday gifts, but occasionally a toy is received.

For refreshments, the children sit at the table which is set with colored paper plates and napkins. For each child there is a *lancia*, an Italian lollypop shaped like an arrow (*lancia* means arrow). Fancy sandwiches of salami, prosciutto, cheeses, and anchovies are served. Chocolates, hard and filled candies, and caramels are favorites with the children. The birthday cake is made of sponge layers that have been sprinkled with rum or coffee flavoring before they are iced with butter cream. *Buon Campleanno* is written across the top of the cake, but there are no candles on it. The children sing the birthday song to the birthday child and he is then given the first slice of cake. It is the Italian version of just the same song used in the United States.

Buon Campleanno a te,	Happy Birthday to you,
Buon Campleanno a te,	Happy Birthday to you,
Buon Campleanno caro	Happy Birthday dear
_____(boys name)_____,	_____(name)_____,
cara	
_____(girl's name)_____,	
Buon Campleanno a te.	Happy Birthday to you.

Plain butter cookies and hot cocoa end the birthday feast.

Caramels

1 cup sugar	1½ cups thin cream
⅔ cup corn syrup	1 teaspoon vanilla

Put sugar, corn syrup, vanilla, and ½ cup cream in a

pan, and stir until sugar dissolves. Boil, stirring gently and constantly, to 234°F. on a candy thermometer, or until mixture forms soft balls when tried in cold water. Add another ½ cup cream. Boil as before, and add remaining cream and boil to 244°F., or until mixture forms decidedly firm ball when tried in cold water. Pour into buttered pan. Cool, cut in squares, and wrap pieces in waxed paper. If sugary when cooled, return to pan, add more cream, and boil again.

Pastini d'Albicocche
(Apricot Cookies)

¼ pound butter
½ cup sugar
3 tablespoons cream
1 egg

2 tablespoons apricot jam
1 cup flour

1 teaspoon baking powder

Cream together butter, sugar, cream, egg, and jam. Sift flour and baking powder into mixture. Mix gently until flour is absorbed. Drop by teaspoonfuls, about 1 inch apart, on greased cooky sheet. Bake in 375°F. (moderate) oven for about 15 minutes, or until light brown. Makes about 1½ dozen.

Pan di Spagna
(Italian Sponge Cake)

5 egg yolks
1½ cups sugar
1¼ cups sifted pastry
    flour

1 teaspoon vanilla
½ teaspoon grated lem-
    on rind
5 egg whites

Beat together egg yolks and sugar in a bowl until lemon colored. Add flour, a little at a time, and blend well. Add vanilla and lemon rind. Beat egg whites until stiff but not dry, and fold into batter. Butter and flour cake pan about 18 inches square. Pour batter in, and bake in 375°F. (moderate) oven for 40 minutes. Turn over on cake rack to cool.

Spumette
(Pink Meringues)

4 egg whites
1 cup powdered sugar

2 drops red vegetable
    coloring

Beat egg whites until frothy. Sift sugar and add to egg whites gradually. Beat until well blended. Add coloring and beat until stiff. Drop by teaspoonfuls onto greased cooky sheet, 1 inch apart. Bake in 375°F. (moderate) oven for 10 minutes, or until puffy and firm.

Remove from oven, cool, and remove from pan with a spatula. Be careful not to crumble meringues. Makes 1½ dozen.

Tortoni

1 egg white	2 tablespoons rum
1 cup heavy cream	4 tablespoons toasted
6 tablespoons confec-	chopped almonds
tioners sugar	

Beat egg whites until stiff, whip cream until foamy, and add sugar gradually. Whip until very stiff. Add rum, beat, and fold in egg white. Pour into 4 medium or 6 small heavy fluted paper cups or chilled molds. Sprinkle with chopped almonds. Place cups in freezing tray, and put in freezing unit, or refrigerate, until firm. Makes 4–6 servings.

Sciroppo di More
(Blackberry Syrup)

1 quart ripe blackberries 3 cups sugar

Wash berries and drain. Place in saucepan with sugar. Cook over low flame about 10 minutes, or until sugar is dissolved and blended into berries. Stir frequently. Use fine sieve to strain. Cool. Keep in airtight jar in cool, dark, dry place.

Mix small quantities of syrup with chilled carbonated water to make the drink.

GAMES

Popular with the six to nine group:

Setaccio
(Sieve)

Children stand in four corners of a square marked on the ground, one in each corner. Another child is IT. IT stands in front of one of the children and says: "May I borrow your sieve?" When he says this, the players in the other three corners must run and exchange places, each going to a new corner. IT and the child he was blocking both try to run to one of the three corners and get there before the other children can exchange. If one of them does, then the child left without a corner becomes IT.

This can be tricky:

Il Cucuzzaro
(The Pumpkin Planter)

One child is IT (the *Cucuzzaro*). The other children are the pumpkins and sit in a circle. Each child is given a number by IT. Standing in the center of the circle IT says: "In my orchard there are 2 pumpkins."

Pumpkin No. 2 must answer: Why 2 pumpkins?

IT: If not, how many?

No. 2: 6 pumpkins.

Then pumpkin No. 6 must answer the same way with another number. The games goes faster and faster. If a player does not answer quickly to his number he must pay a silly penalty (see page 187).

THE GIGGLERS are always set off by this one:

Cencio Mollo
(The Wet Handkerchief)

One child is IT. The other players form a line. Holding a handkerchief in his hand, IT says to the first player in the line: "The wet handkerchief has come to you."

The first child must answer: "Let it come. I shall not laugh, cry, nor kiss it."

IT tries to make the child laugh. He can touch his face or head *only* with the handkerchief. IT continues this from player to player in the line. Any child who laughs must pay a penalty (see page 187).

Girotonto
(Ring Around)

This is the Italian name for Ring Around a Rosie.

Campanaro
(Bell Tower)

Hopscotch, played with an orange peel.

A FAVORITE game with boys:

Morra

Two or more can play. The players pair off, and each makes a fist with one hand. There is no signal to start the game, but the players simultaneously start stretching out the fingers of the clenched fist, one finger after the next. Before the fingers are all quite out, both players call a number between 2 and 10. If the number called by one of the contestants corresponds to the sum of the number of fingers extended by both contestants, a point is scored by the correct caller.

The game may be played by teams, with each player paired against another on the opposite team. If there are four or less on a team, six points may constitute a game. With more than four players, twelve points may decide the tilt.

Trentuno
(Thirty-one)

Hide and Seek. IT must count to 31 before he looks for the hidden children (see Game Directory).

Pesta

This is the name for Tag (see Game Directory).

Musical Chairs
(see Game Directory)

The birthday child is allowed to have his own way as much as possible on his birthday and occasionally as a special treat he may be taken to see a movie by his parents.

Japan

THE BIRTHDAY party has become a part of Japanese culture since World War II. The Japanese birthday party is usually celebrated at home with the family and close relatives and friends invited by the birthday child's mother. The house is not especially decorated, but the child is outfitted in brand new clothes for the occasion.

Guests are greeted *Mashi-Mashi* (Hello) and they wish the birthday child *Tanzobi Omedeto* (Happy Birthday) as they arrive. Gifts of clothes or toys are given to younger children. Money is presented to an older child. *Arigato* (Thank you), the birthday child tells each giver. To request a special gift, or even to indicate a preference, is considered impolite among the Japanese.

116

Sometimes a birthday cake is purchased for the party. It says Happy Birthday on the top and is decorated with floral designs. The first slice is presented to the birthday child. More important than a birthday cake is *Osekihan.* This is a rice dish mixed with beans. Or *Osushi,* which is rice mixed with vegetables and seasoned with vinegar. Japanese tea or a punch are the favored drinks at birthday parties for guests of any age.

The Japanese recipes that follow are good for an evening supper party for older children.

Osekihan
(Red Beans and Rice)

1½ cups dried kidney beans	1 cup raw rice
2 teaspoons salt	3 tablespoons soy sauce

2 tablespoons saké (rice wine) or dry sherry

Wash the beans. Cover with water and bring to a boil. Remove from the heat and let stand 1 hour. Drain. Add fresh water to cover and 1 teaspoon salt. Bring to a boil. Cover and cook over low heat for 1 hour, or until tender.

Wash the rice in several changes of water. Add 2½ cups water and remaining teaspoon salt. Cover, bring to a boil, and cook over low heat 20 minutes, or until tender. Drain. Combine with the beans, soy sauce, and saké or sherry. Mix lightly. Cover and cook over low heat until dry, about 5 minutes. Serves 6 to 8.

Sukiyaki

¾ pound beef sirloin	Salad oil
1 green pepper	Salt
3 green onions or scallions	Sugar
	Soy sauce
3 tomatoes	Cooked rice
Cornstarch	

Slice the meat into paper-thin 2-inch strips, cutting against the grain. Cut the green pepper into strips and the green onions into 1-inch pieces. Cut the tomatoes into eighths. Dust the meat with cornstarch and set aside.

Put a very little oil in a skillet and cook the green pepper in it until slightly wilted. Add the onion and cook a little more. Empty cooked vegetables into a serving dish and keep warm. Put more oil in the pan, add the tomatoes, sprinkle with salt, and sugar, and heat quickly, letting them stay firm. Empty into the dish. Brown the meat quickly in the skillet, with soy sauce to moisten. Empty the meat into the dish with the vegetables and toss all together lightly. Serve over rice. Serves 6.

Katsetura
(Japanese Sponge Cake)

5 eggs	¾ teaspoon double-
⅔ cup sugar	action baking powder
¼ cup honey	2 tablespoons confec-
¾ cup sifted flour	tioners' sugar

Preheat the oven to 350°F. Oil an 8-inch brownie pan or a 9-inch by 12-inch loaf pan, and dust lightly with flour.

Beat eggs until light, then add sugar and honey. Beat until thick (about 10 minutes). Sift the flour and baking powder into the mixture; beat only until smooth. Turn into the pan. Bake 40 minutes, or until a cake tester comes out clean. Cool on cake rack 10 minutes, then turn out onto the cake rack until completely cool. Turn right side up and sprinkle with confectioners' sugar. Serves 10–12.

Oriental Punch

1 cup sugar	¼ cup lemon juice
1 cup water	1 cup orange juice
6 cloves	1 drop oil of pepper-
1-inch stick cinnamon	mint
½ tablespoon chopped	Green vegetable coloring
crystalized ginger	Fresh mint

119

Boil sugar and water 5 minutes. Add cloves, cinnamon, and ginger. Cover and let stand until cold. Add fruit juices, strain, and add peppermint oil and a few drops of green coloring. Let stand 1 hour, and pour into a punch bowl over a cake of ice. Garnish with fresh mint leaves.

Origami, the art of folding paper, is a well-known handcraft in Japan; it has been practiced for over ten centuries. It is learned by young children and is very often taught in the schools. Animals, human shapes, flowers, and inanimate objects are made of bright-colored thin pieces of paper which are always square in shape. Paper folded in bird shapes may be given to the birthday child as the bird is a symbol of good luck.

Paper Fan

Accordion pleat a 6-inch wide and 30-inch long piece of stiff colored paper. Use designed paper, or first draw your own designs on white paper and color them. Hold pleats all folded together, and fold one end up about 1 inch. Wrap this end with colored tape to use as a handle. The fans makes good party favors for girls.

GAMES

Fuku-warai

Otafuku is a good-natured Japanese goddess who is always smiling. Her name means Goddess of Fortune and she is especially popular because her motto is "Laugh and grow fat."

Draw a large outline of the head of Otafuku. Paint on only her hair. Cut out paper eyebrows, eyes, nose, ears, and mouth in appropriate colors. Make the shapes very definite, as this is a blindfolded game. Blindfold a child and, with one hand behind his back, he must try to place the features on Otafuku correctly.

Otadama
(Bean Bags)

This is the juggling of bean bags to see who can juggle the most bags for the longest time.

Bean Bags

Small pieces of felt in several colors   Dried beans

Sew two 5-inch circles of felt together. Use two different colors, stitch close to the edge, and leave an opening about 1½ inches wide. Turn bag inside out, and fill with about ½ cup of beans. Stitch remaining opening to close the bag. Trim top of bag with other bits of differently colored felt cut in designs or figures. Paste on with fabric cement, or sew on. These make good favors for boys and can be used for games or juggling at the party.

Hanetsuki

For ten players or more. Use two large toy balloons. Players divide into two equal groups. Each group forms its own circle and has its own balloon. At the signal the balloon is batted into the air. The object is to hit the balloon with the open hand, keeping it up in the air and not letting it touch the ground. The group that keeps it in the air longest wins.

Rakan-san

Rakan was an ancient Buddhist priest. *San* is an affectionate suffix. He was supposed to have had an odd-looking face.

The players sit in a circle, each facing slightly to the right, so he can observe the player on his right. The leader calls: "Let's all imitate a Rakan-san pose. One, two three . . . POSE!" Each player strikes a pose (hand on eyes, arms in a funny position, etc.). After a few seconds, the leader repeats the phrase again, only this time each player must pose as the person to his right had just been posing. As the game speeds up it becomes increasingly difficult to shift positions quickly and the results are very funny.

Hanakago
(The Flower Basket)

Ten to thirty may play. Players are seated in a circle with one player, who is IT, standing in the center. Cushions or chairs are used for seats. There must be a seat for each player except IT.

Each player is given the name of a flower (Cherry Blossom, Aster, and so on). IT calls the names of any two flowers. The players representing those flowers must change seats. In the scramble, IT tries to get a seat. The player left out becomes IT, and the game continues. If IT calls *"Hanakago,"* then all the players must change seats.

Kick the Can

Four or more can play. A circle about 4 feet in diameter is drawn with chalk. In the center of this circle in an empty can. One player is IT. The can is kicked out of the circle. IT must retrieve it and place it back in the center of the circle. As soon as the can is kicked, all the other players run and hide. IT tries to find them. When he spies a player, he calls his name and dashes for the can. If he beats the hider to it, that person becomes a prisoner. If he does not, that player kicks the can and runs and hides again. Any hider may rush in and kick the can if he can beat IT to it. The game continues until IT has caught all the hidden children. Then IT is replaced, with the first player who was caught becoming the new IT.

Japanese Tag

Four or more can play. The one who it IT tries to tag a player. However, the tagged player must put one hand on the spot touched by the chaser, whether the back, the shoulder, the elbow, knee, or any other part of the body. In this position he must chase the other players. He is relieved of his position only when he tags another player. (In Brazil, this same version of Tag is called Sick Cat, which is a good description of how IT sometimes looks.)

Kage-bohi-migo
(Shadow Game)

The children chase after each other trying to step on each others shadows.

Tops

Japanese tops are all gaily painted, some are tops within tops, others play a little tune as they spin; see Mail Order Shopping Directory.

Kites

Japanese children love to fly their very colorful kites. Many authentic kites at various prices can be bought at the "Go Fly a Kite" store; see Mail Order Shopping Directory.

Puzzles

All sorts of puzzles are popular with Japanese children, too; see Mail Order Shopping Directory.

The most important birthdays are the third, fifth, and seventh years. On these years the child and his family go to the local shrine and give thanks and offer prayers. In Japan there is also a special day set aside for girls and one for boys. These days are considered of equal, or greater, importance than the celebration of one's own birthday, with the exception of the third, fifth, and seventh. March 3rd is Girls' Day. This is the day of the doll festival. Elaborate dolls, dressed to represent court figures of ancient times, are displayed and may be played with. These dolls have been in the family for many years and may have been the treasured possessions of a great-great-grandmother. May 5th is Boy's Day. Large cloth or paper carp are flown from poles in front of each house that has a son. Carp are the symbol of strength and courage in boys. The father puts the carp on a pole outside his house in the hope that his son will display these qualities.

Mexico

MEXICAN families give two parties if the actual birthday and the Saint's Name Day do not fall on the same date. Both parties are usually all-day affairs, the only difference being that the entire family and their guests attend church together on the Name Day and the priest blesses the child during the service.

Party invitations, with an appropriate picture and verse, are occasionally used to invite the guests to the festivities at the birthday child's home. The house is decorated with balloons, streamers, and flowers. Colored paper plates and napkins, party hats, blowers, and paper baskets make the party table gay. Mexican families have five meals each day, and when a birthday party is given guests ordinarily join the family for the entire day and partake of all meals. Breakfast (*desa-*

yuno) is served in the morning, brunch *(almuerzo)* is a mid-morning snack, lunch *(comida)* is the main meal of the day, snack time *(merienda)* tides one over until dinner *(cena)*, which is the final meal of the day.

Guests arrive early in the morning on the day of the celebration, dressed in their best party clothes.¡Hola! (Hello) they are greeted. *Feliz Cumpleaños* (Happy Birthday) echoes throughout the house and as the gifts of toys and clothes are received, the birthday child says *Gracias* (Thank you) to gift givers. Everyone admires the birthday cards with pictures and verses, that the birthday child has received.

The round layered birthday cake, covered with whipped cream and decorated with flowers and Happy Birthday to ——(name)—— written across the top, is served at the breakfast. Candles, one for each year of life, circle the top of the cake and are blown out by the birthday child after he has made three secret wishes. The first slice of cake is served to him and the birthday song is sung in his honor.

Estes son las mañanitas	These are early mornings
Que cantaba el rey David	King David used to sing
A las muchachas bonitas	To the pretty girls
Se las cantamos aqui	We sing it here
Despierta mi bien	Wake up my darling
despierta	wake up
Mira que ya amanecio	Morning has came

Ya los pajaritos cantan	The birds are already singing
La luna ya se metio.	The moon has set.

Tortas, which are hard rolls with soft insides, are served for brunch. They are oblong in shape and have thick centers and taper towards the ends. Any type of filling is put into the *tortas. Tacos* (the Mexican sandwich) is another brunch favorite. They are made of *tortillas* that are rolled up after being filled with meat, poultry, or any other desired type of filling. The *tortilla* is a thin, round cornmeal pancake. Luncheon, which is the main meal of the day, customarily consists of *enchilades* (thin, round corn-flour pancakes filled with chicken and rolled up) with *mole* (a thick dark-brown, hot sauce made of hot peppers and a little dark bitter chocolate melted in, and with peanuts and almonds ground into it) and grated cheese and onions sprinkled on top. At snacktime, more *tortas* or *tacos* are eaten. Dinner consists of *tamales.* (Corn flour mixed with water, milk, and seasoning makes a paste that is rolled around a stuffing. This is then rolled inside a corn husk and boiled. The mixture cooks up hard and is removed from the husk; it then has the shape of a banana.) *Atole* (boiled milk with flour and sugar in it) is a hot drink for the children, while adults drink *pulque* (an alcoholic beverage made from the Maguey cactus). There are also cold drinks and a choice of Mexican sweets.

Dulce de Piloncillo
(Mexican Brown Sugar Candy)

1 cup brown sugar	1½ teaspoons butter
¼ cup water	½ cup broken pecans
1½ teaspoons vinegar	or walnut meats

Mix together brown sugar, water, vinegar, and butter in a saucepan. Stir and cook over low heat about 15 minutes, until syrup thickens and spins a thread when dropped from a spoon into cold water. Add the nuts. Remove from heat and beat until creamy. Drop from spoon onto waxed paper and let cool. Makes about 10 candies.

Huevitos de Faltriquera
(Colonial Candy Eggs)

2 cups sugar	¼ teaspoon powdered
1 cup water	clove
8 egg yolks, beaten	Powdered sugar
4 ounces almonds,	Waxed paper
blanched and ground	Colored tissue paper
½ teaspoon cinnamon	

Boil together sugar and water until syrup forms a thread when dropped from a spoon (about 15 minutes). Cool, and add beaten egg yolks, almonds, cinnamon, and clove. Cook over low heat about 10 minutes, stirring constantly. Remove from heat and stir until firm.

Spread powdered sugar lightly on a plate. Turn mixture onto sugar. Mold into small balls, and wrap each ball in waxed paper and then in colored tissue paper. Makes about 2 dozen small eggs.

Bolitas de Nuez
(Pecan Candy)

2 cups ground pecans
1 cup powdered sugar

2 egg whites, beaten
stiffly

Mix pecans with sugar, and add beaten egg whites. Form mixture into small balls. Bake on a buttered baking sheets in 350°F. (moderate) oven for 5 minutes. Makes about 16 candies.

Mantecados
(Butter Cakes)

½ pound butter
1 cup sugar
6 eggs

2 cups flour, sifted
2 tablespoons
powdered sugar

Cream together butter and sugar. One by one add the eggs, and beat after adding each, then add flour gradually. Beat until very smooth. Pour into 2 dozen muffin tins lined with paper cups. Sprinkle with powdered sugar. Bake in 375°F. (moderately hot) oven for 15 to 20 minutes. Makes 4 dozen cakes.

Naquis
(Miniature Doughnuts)

1 egg	⅓ cup buttermilk
½ cup sugar	2 cups sifted flour
Pinch baking soda	Fat for deep frying
½ teaspoon salt	

Mix together all ingredients, forming a soft dough. Add more milk if necessary. Roll and shape by hand into tiny doughnuts. Fry in hot deep fat (350°F.) and drain on brown paper. Makes 3 dozen.

Panecillos
(Round Cookies)

2 cups sifted flour	¼ cup olive oil
½ cup sugar	¼ cup chopped seedless
1 egg	raisins
1 tablespoon lemon juice	½ cup chopped pecans

Mix together flour, sugar, egg, lemon juice, olive oil, and chopped raisins to form a smooth dough. Mold into small balls about the size of walnuts, and place on greased cooky sheets. Sprinkle with pecans and additional sugar. Bake in 350°F. (moderate) oven for 20 to 25 minutes. Makes about 3 dozen.

Chicha
(Pineappleade)

1 small fresh pineapple	½ teaspoon powdered
1 pound sugar	clove
3 quarts water	¼ teaspoon powdered
3 sliced limes	nutmeg
1 teaspoon cinnamon	

Wash pineapple well. Peel, and chop the peeling; grind the pulp. Dissolve sugar in water, add limes, ground pulp, chopped peeling, and spices. Let stand in covered earthenware or enamel jug for 24 hours or longer. Strain and chill. Makes 4 quarts.

Chicha de Limón
(Mexican Lemonade)

3 small fresh pineapples	1 tablespoon powdered
24 lemons	cinnamon
2 pounds sugar	Pinch powdered clove

Wash pineapple, then chop finely, skins and all. Add juice of 24 lemons, and sugar, cinnamon, and clove. Stir well, let stand overnight, and next day add more sugar to taste. Color pink with pomegranate juice (grenadine) or currant or grape juice. Strain through fine sieve, cool, and serve with ice.

GAMES

An EXCITING game:

Coyote and Sheep

Eight to twelve can play. One player is the Shepherd, one the Coyote, and the rest are sheep. The sheep and Shepherd form a line, one behind the other, each with hands clasped around the waist of the player in front of him. The Shepherd is at the head of the line. The Coyote approaches, and the Shepherd asks: "What does the coyote want?"

The Coyote answers: I want fat meat!

The Shepherd calls: Then go to the end of the line where the fattest sheep are.

When the Shepherd says this, the Coyote breaks for the end of the line to try to tag the last sheep. The Shepherd defends his flock by extending his arms and running in all directions trying to prevent the Coyote from getting to the last sheep. The line of sheep also helps by weaving back and forth. The sheep and Shepherd must not break their line. If they do, the Shepherd becomes the next Coyote and the next man in line becomes the Shepherd. The same thing is true when the Coyote tags the last player in line.

Juan Pirulero
(John the Piccolo)

The children sit in a circle with the leader in the center. He pretends to play an instrument (guitar, violin, flute, piano, harp) and the other children pretend to play instruments, too, but *not* the one he is playing. At intervals, he changes his instrument and anyone in the circle who is playing his new choice must switch to a different one. If any of the players forgets to change, or it too slow in doing so, he is out. As they play this game, Mexican children chant:

Este es el juego	This is the game
De Juan Pirulero y cada	Of John the Piccolo and everyone
Quien atiende a su juego.	Pays attention to this game.

A GOOD outdoor game:

Encantados
(Enchanted)

A home base is chosen (a tree or an area of ground where the players are "safe"), and one child is IT. The children run from the home base to tease IT. If he tags one, the player must remain in that spot until someone from the home base runs out and tags him free again, without getting tagged himself.

La Gallina Ciega
(The Blind Hen)

Played like Blindman's Buff (see Game Directory).

Sacos

A sack race (see Game Directory).

Le Rueda de San Miguel
(The Wheel of San Miguel)

Played like London Bridge (see Game Directory), but in the Mexican version there is no Tug-of-War at the end.

Colores
(Colors)

The players are all seated. There is a leader, who may be an adult as he does not really participate in the game. A safety area is marked out some distance from the group. The leader appoints a Devil and an Angel and also secretly assigns a color to each of the other players. Then the Devil pretends to knock on the leader's door.

Leader asks: What do you want?
Devil: A ribbon.
Leader: What color?
Devil: (Names a color).

At this point, the child who has been assigned that color gets up and runs from the Devil, who tries to catch him. If he is caught before he reaches the safety area, he must join the Devil. If not, he can rejoin the group. Next, the Angel repeats what the Devil did. When no one is left, the game is over and the one that has captured the most children wins.

Roña

This is the Mexican name for Tag (see Game Directory).

Storytelling is a feature of the Mexican birthday party. *Snow White, Cinderella, Sleeping Beauty, Red Riding Hood, The Enchanted Princess,* and *The Wizard of Oz* are some of the familiar fairy tales that the children look forward to hearing.

The climax of the Mexican birthday party is the *piñata.* This is a clay bowl filled with candies, nuts, or toys that is covered with papier-mâché and molded by hand into a shape and allowed to dry hard. It is then covered with many strips of colored frilled paper that are pasted in place. The final shape looks like a bull, rooster, lamb or any animal or fantastic shape. The *piñata* is hung from the ceiling and each child gets a chance to try to open it. Each child is blindfolded when it is his turn and given a big stick with which to hit the *piñata* and try to crack it open. When it is finally broken, the goodies come showering down and all the children share them. To make a *piñata*, see page 42.

The birthday song is sung in school to the birthday child. His friends bring him small gifts and try to give him *chetes* (spanks), one for each year of life. Mexicans do not seem to mind the custom of having teenage girls serenaded by their friends at 5 A.M. on the mornings of their birthdays. (I wonder how kindly neighbors take to this?) When a Mexican girl is fifteen years old, a large party, a birthday ball, is given for her. This is to introduce her officially to society and to announce that she is now a young lady. On this day she may stay home from school. As special privileges Mexican children do not have to do their chores on the day of their celebration and they may stay up later than their customary bedtime.

New Zealand

THE CHILDREN in New Zealand like to have their birthday cakes topped with a special decoration illustrating their favorite hobby or sport. Girls tend to favor a small celluloid ballerina, a favorite animal, or small colorful umbrellas. Boys' cakes feature a ball player, missiles, a swimmer, or a toy car or truck.

Relatives and school and neighborhood friends are invited to birthday parties given at home for most New Zealand children until they are about twelve. Colored paper napkins and streamers are used to make the party table festive. Each setting has a paper hat, squeaker (noisemaker), and balloon. Occasionally small favors are provided, too.

Place Cards and Mats

Cut colored construction paper into cards 2 inches by 3½ inches. Decorate on the top left side with a motif or design that will be the theme of the party table. It can be a painted design. Or glue on small seashells to make flowers or a stylized decoration. Designs cut from several colors of felt and glued on are bright and effective, too. Print guest's name in ink on center of card.

Matching placemats are made by using pieces of construction paper 10 inches by 15 inches and decorating them with the same motif, but larger than on the cards.

An iced fruit cake is served as the birthday cake, with Happy Birthday, or Greetings, written across the top in addition to the special miniature-toy decoration. Lighted candles ring the cake, and the same Happy Birthday song we know is sung as the cake is brought in and the first slice is cut for the birthday child.

Guests bring inexpensive gifts, but something they feel the child would enjoy.

GAMES

Hunt the Slipper

This is especially popular as an outdoor game, and it is

the same HOT and COLD seeking game known in so many countries (see Hide the Object, page 80).

FOR YOUNG children:

Black Magic

Two adults lead this demonstration of black magic.

One adult holds a magic wand. His partner knows that, when he points in a certain way with the wand, the object pointed to is the answer. The children do not know of this arrangement. The partner leaves the room and the children choose an object. When the partner returns, he tries to guess what the object is. Of course, he watches the adult with the wand and is able to name the correct item when the wand finally points to it.

Many of the games played in England and Australia are well-known in New Zealand. Group singing of popular songs is always enjoyed at parties. Teenagers are more likely to have a few friends in to dinner at home and to finish off the celebration by going to the movies rather than having a traditional birthday party. Kindergarteners have Happy Birthday sung to them by their classmates, but the upper classes usually make no fuss over birthdays. Younger children have the usual special privilege of staying up late to add to the fun of having a birthday. The twenty-first birthday is the important one in New Zealand, when the child is thereafter considered an adult.

Philippines

A CHILD in the Philippines always goes to hear Mass with his parents and brothers and sisters on his birthday. He receives Holy Communion on this day and gives his thanks to God. He or she is all dressed in new clothes, from hair ribbons to shoes.

Very early in the morning on the day of the celebration, relatives arrive at the house to help the birthday child's mother prepare the feast to be served to the party guests. Sometimes the celebration is a family gathering with all the relatives spending the day. Other times a special party is held for both relatives and friends who have been invited by phone or by invitation cards.

The birthday party is held at home, usually from 4 to 10 P.M. As the guests enter the gate, they see balloons of different colors, with greetings and the date of the birthday printed on them, strung around the garden, and there are also colored lights blinking on and off to make the garden festive as evening comes.

Birthday Balloons

Blow up lots of balloons of different colors, and with wide felt marking pens write on them, Happy Birthday to ——— (name) ——— and the date of the birthday.

Maligayang Kaarawan (Happy Birthday in the language called Tagalog) each guest greets the birthday child and kisses him. *Salamat* (Thank you) the child responds as he is handed a gift. Coloring books, pencils, tops, and books are usually received from friends, while parents give money, jewelry, new clothes, or more expensive toys. In return for the gifts, the birthday child hands each guest a balloon, a bag of candy, and a party horn to blow.

On the table are colored paper or plastic plates and napkins with colorful flower designs on them. Soft candies, fancy cookies and cookies in the shapes of animals, cold drinks, and ice cream are served. When everyone has arrived, the birthday child stands on a stool in front of the birthday cake and all the guests surround him. The visitors sing Happy Birthday and the child then blows out all his candles and gets the first slice. Most birthday cakes are sponge or butter cakes covered with icing. Sometimes an ice-cream cake (cake and ice cream in layers) in the shape of a ship or doll or airplane and decorated with icing and different colored candles is used.

Coconut Balls

1 cup sugar   3 cups flaked coconut
⅓ cup water

Boil the sugar and water until a thread is formed when a fork is dipped in and raised. Stir in the coconut and cook over low heat, stirring frequently until a soft ball is formed when a little of the mixture is dropped into cold water. Drop by the tablespoon onto a greased surface. Cool. Makes 36 balls.

GAMES

Pusa at Aso
(Cat and Dog)

This game can be played indoors or out. There are ten to twelve players. All the players except one are cats. They sit in a circle around a pile of shoes, sticks, stones, or other objects which represent a pile of bones. One player is chosen to be the dog, and he sits inside the circle guarding his bones. He cannot move around. He can only tag the cats by touching them from where he sits with his hands or feet. The cats try to steal the bones without being tagged. If the dog tags a cat, they exchange places. If the cats get all the bones without being tagged, a new game starts with the same dog.

A BOYS' game:

Forcing the Gates

For ten or more players. Two lines are formed, each with an equal number of players. The lines stand facing each other, about 10 feet to 15 feet apart. The players in each line hold hands.

A player runs out from one team and dashes with all his might against the hands of his opponents. If he breaks through, he takes back to his side the two players whose clasped hands he separated. If he fails to break through, he has to join his opponents. Then a player from the other side attempts to "force the gates." This continues until one side has no one left.

Puss in the Circle

For four or more players. A circle 4 to 6 feet in diameter is marked on the ground. One player, who is

Puss, stands in the center of the circle. The other players stand outside the circle, surrounding it. The object is for Puss to tag the other players, which he can do only when they take a chance and put one foot inside the circle. If someone pretends to start putting his foot in, that may distract Puss and another player may get his foot in and out again without getting tagged. Anyone whom Puss catches becomes a prisoner and helps Puss tag the others.

Lame Duck

A tag game for four or more players. Players scatter about the space, which is decided upon in advance. One player is the Lame Duck, and all the players must stay inside the game area. The Lame Duck hops on one foot and tries to tag the other players. When he succeeds, the player caught becomes the next Lame Duck and the game continues.

Potato Joust

For two or any even number of players. Two players face each other, about 3 feet apart. Each player kneels and holds one leg up off the floor by the ankle with one hand. In the other hand he has a potato firmly jabbed on the prongs of a fork. Each player tries to knock his opponent's potato off the fork, at the same time protecting his own. A slight turn of the wrist, a quick push, and a potato is flying. A player is defeated if 1) he loses his potato, or 2) if he topples over three times. If he lets go of his ankle in order to keep his balance, this is considered a fall.

Stoop Tag

For five or more players. Players scatter over the playing area with one player being IT. IT chases the others, trying to tag one of them. A player may escape being tagged by stooping or squatting. However, each player may stoop only *three* times while any one player is IT. After that he may escape only by running. Any player tagged become IT.

Teenagers invite their own friends and classmates to their parties. They make their own invitations and greeting cards. Invitations are often made of colored paper cut in a circle and decorated to look like a phonograph record, for social dancing and group singing will be part of the fun at the party as well as games. The Twist and many other new dances are very popular in the Philippines.

At school, teacher and classmates sing Happy Birthday to the birthday child in class. At recess, he pays for a treat at the canteen for his classmates. This is called "a blow out," and they feast on ice cream, candy, and cookies.

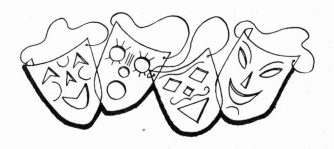

Russia

IN RUSSIA, the birthday pie with Happy Birthday pricked into the crust is just as popular as a birthday cake. The Russian child awakens to find his family's gifts near his bed on the morning of his birthday. Party guests are invited personally or are sent invitations to an afternoon party that is given at home. If they cannot attend, friends send birthday cards, which have an appropriate picture and verse, to extend their good wishes.

The house is festively decorated with balloons and streamers. Party hats, masks, and sometimes inexpensive favors are provided for each child at his place at the table.

Paper Masks

Cut a rectangular piece of strong wrapping paper large enough to cover the face and extend as far as the ears on each side. Hold against face and mark position of eyes, nose, and mouth. Cut eye holes, a triangle for the nose, and a slit for the mouth. Paint on funny eyebrows and a big red circle on each cheek. For boys' masks you could add a bushy black moustache made of wool, and for girls attach braids of yellow wool on each side of the mask. Punch holes near the top on either side of mask, reinforce holes with tape so they will not tear, and tie strings through the holes, which later will be tied behind child's head to hold the mask on.

Zdravstvuyte (Hello) the birthday child greets his friends, and they all wish him *S Dnem Rojdeniya* (Happy Birthday) as they arrive. Friends customarily bring gifts of toys or books, while parents often give clothes as well. *Spasibo* (Thank you) each gift giver is told.

The birthday party is customarily a special tea, although sometimes a dinner party is held. Any type of food that the birthday child particularly likes is served. Usually sandwiches, all kinds of candy, fruit, pastries, cake, tea, coffee or any other preferred drink are offered. Any type of fancy cake is used as the birthday cake. Happy Birthday ———(name)——— is written across the top and candles, one for each year, circle it. But a birthday pie is just as popular and is often used instead. The first slice is always given to the birthday child.

Russian Tea Cakes

½ pound soft butter
½ cup sifted confection-
  ers' sugar
1 teaspoon vanilla

2¼ cups sifted cake
  flour
¼ teaspoon salt
¾ cup finely chopped
  nuts

Cream together thoroughly the butter, sugar, and vanilla. Sift together the flour and salt, and stir into butter mixture, then stir in nuts. Chill dough. Roll dough into 1-inch balls, and place 2½ inches apart on ungreased baking sheet. Bake until set but not brown. While still warm, roll in more confectioners' sugar. Cool, and roll in sugar again. Now bake 10 to 12 minutes in 400°F. (moderately hot) oven. Makes about 4 dozen.

GAMES

Gorelki
(Widower, or Last Couple Out)

Nine or more can play. Players line up by couples. The extra player, IT, stands from 6 to 10 feet in front of the head couple, with his back to them. When IT shouts "Last couple out," that couple must leave the rear and move forward with the idea of passing IT and joining hands in front of him. They must come up on either side of the two lines of players and not on the same side. IT may not turn his head to see them coming, he must look straight ahead. Only when they get even with him may he leave his place. When they do get even with him, he dashes after one of them to try to tag the player before the couple can join hands in front of him. If IT succeeds, the player tagged takes his place as IT, the first IT and the other member of the couple become the head couple, and the new IT tries his luck. If IT doesn't tag anyone before the couple joins hands, this couple becomes the head couple and the last couple in line continue the game.

Karavai
(*The Round Loaf*)

This is a verse game that is acted out. The children join hands and encircle the birthday child, who is the first IT. For the first two lines they walk around him; on the third line they drop hands and as they continue the verse they act out the words with their arms, still marching around the circle. They join hands again, and during the last line, at "someone special," the birthday

child picks another child in the circle to take his place
and the game continues.

On ——— (name's) ——— birthday
We bake a round loaf,
So wide,   (motion with arms)
So high,   ("   "   "   )
So low,   ("   "   "   )
So narrow, ("   "   "   )
       (Now the children clasp hands again)
Round loaf, round loaf,
Let him who wishes take some.
I love you all,
But *someone special* more than all!

Other games we know are Hide and Seek (see Game
Directory) and Lottos (like Bingo). Russian children
also love to be shown magic tricks. Prizes of cookies or
inexpensive toys are given to game winners. Occasionally children go to a movie or a puppet show as
a birthday treat.

Kindergarten children very often receive a small
birthday gift from their teacher and handmade presents are occasionally presented by their classmates. In
higher grades, the teacher congratulates the birthday
child and a special class committee arranges for a sur-
prise gift (such as flowers) as a token from all his
classmates.

The sixteenth birthday in Russia is celebrated with an evening party and dance. The eighteenth year is voting age but the twenty-first birthday is the one recognized as the real coming of age.

Scotland

Scottish children are given "punches" by their friends on their birthdays, one punch for each year and one to grow on. Children's birthdays are celebrated with cards, gifts, and a simple afternoon party at home for the child and his friends. The guests are invited personally; invitations are not sent out.

Neither the house nor the party table are especially decorated for a birthday, but the cake is quite elaborate. It is a large round cake of one layer covered with marzipan and frosted with white icing which is put on top of that. Happy Birthday is written across the top of the cake in colored icing and flowers made of icing are added for further decoration. There are candles on the cake, too, one for each year, and the birthday child makes his secret wish and blows them out. The first slice goes to him. Scottish children sing the same birthday song as children in the United States do.

Small pastries, biscuits (cookies), ice cream, soft candy sugar squares of different colors, and little round colored sugar balls known as Dolly Mixtures are served to the guests. Ginger is the popular drink at birthday parties; ginger is the name for soda of any flavor.

Toys are the usual gifts received, not clothes or money.

Marzipan

¼ pound blanched almonds

¼ pound confectioners' sugar

1 egg white, beaten

¼ teaspoon salt

Grind almonds fine in food grinder. Mix together all ingredients and knead smooth. If paste is too stiff, it may be softened with a very little lemon juice. Let stand for 24 hours, covered, before using.

Glossy White Icing

1½ cups sugar

½ cup milk

Combine sugar and milk and heat gently until sugar dissolves and mixture blends and thickens a bit. Remove from heat, beat well with a spoon, and spread on cake.

GAMES

Wee Bologne Man

This is very like the game called Adam Had Seven Sons that is played in England. There are six or more players. A leader stands in front of them and says:

I'm the Wee Bologne Man,
Always do the best you can
To follow the Wee Bologne Man.

Then he goes through the motions of playing some instrument in a band (violin, cymbals, drum, etc.), or he can make any motions he wants. The rest of the players must follow suit. Each time he changes to a new movement, he must repeat the rhyme. As the game proceeds, the pace quickens and those unable to follow are out. At any time the leader may pick another leader by pointing to him or calling his name and they exchange places.

Musical Chairs
(see Game Directory)

Blindman's Buff
(see Game Directory)

London Bridge
(see Game Directory)

Dusty Bluebells

This is the same game as In and Out the Window, page 81, that is played in Iceland.

Hot Potato
(see Game Directory)

Hide the Object
(see page 80)

Prizes are not given to game winners at Scottish parties. The children do not have a birthday celebration in their schools, but at home the birthday child is usually allowed to have his way all during the day.

The fifteenth birthday is special in Scotland as it is the year that children are allowed to leave school. The twenty-first birthday is considered the most important and that party is often held in a hired hall. It is the year that the birthday celebrant gets his "key to the house," as in done in England and Ireland, to show that he is considered an adult and is free to come and go as he pleases without consulting his parents. Greeting cards sent for the twenty-first birthday have a silver key at the top in honor of the occasion.

South Africa

BECAUSE of the fine warm climate of South Africa, most children's parties are held outdoors on the lawn or on the veranda, in the afternoon. Except for flowers, special decorations are not customary. A picnic table is set out under the trees and the children sit on the lawn and eat buffet style. A linen cloth covers the table and cloth napkins and china dishes are used. For each child there is a paper basket filled with candies. The baskets are made by hand by the family especially for the party. Each child also receives a balloon.

Paper Candy Basket

Use a colored party paper napkin; this works best when the paper is not too soft or thick. Fold the four corners of the napkin toward the center in pie-shaped wedges so that they meet in the center. Repeat the same process again, on the same side; then repeat again once more on this side. Now turn napkin over to other side. Repeat corner-folding process *once* on this side. Turn back over to first side, and place on top of a drinking glass. Now gently pull down all four corner pockets, then pull down the second and third layers of corner pockets underneath, one after the other. Remove from glass to find a neatly formed candy container.

The guests are greeted with *Goeie Middag* (Good afternoon), and they say to the birthday child, Many Happy Returns of the Day, or, in the Afrikaans language, *Veels geluk op jou Verjaarsdag* (Good wishes on your birthday), and he replies *Baie dankie* (Thank you).

The birthday cake is a fruit cake thickly frosted with a soft almond-flavored icing and a hard, white sugar icing on top of that. Happy Birthday —— (name) —— is written across the top of the cake, which is baked by the child's mother weeks in advance, as it takes quite a while to prepare. Birthday candles circle the fruit cake, one for each year, and the birthday child is given the first slice after making his secret wish and blowing out the candles. The birthday song is the same as the one sung in the United States. Besides the birthday cake, cookies and many varieties of mixed candies are served. Ice cream, puddings (any dessert other than ice cream or "jelly" is called a pudding), and jellies (any flavor of gelatin) are offered. Lemonade (this term is used for any flavor of soda) and Coke are popular party drinks. And a trifle is a must at South African birthday parties.

South African Trifle

Pour a layer of half-cooled custard into a serving bowl, and, before the custard thickens, cut into it pieces of sponge cake soaked in sherry or other flavoring. After this thickens, a layer of whipped cream with maraschino cherries and nuts is put on. The layers are repeated for as many as desired. The trifle is topped with a final layer of whipped cream and decorated with cherries and nuts.

GAMES

GAMES are usually played first at South African birthday parties, before the children are served refreshments.

Early Rose

Two lines are formed, one of girls and one of boys. An extra boy, IT, stands at the front of the lines and calls: Early Rose! The first girl and boy then run to the end of their respective lines. IT tries to catch the girl before she can get to the end of her line. If he does, he then can take her partner's place in the boys' line and her partner becomes IT.

Knikkertjie
(*Winking Game*)

A wide circle of girls is formed, facing in. Within that circle, another circle of their boy partners is formed, facing out toward the girls. An extra boy, IT, stands in the center of both circles. IT winks at a girl, and she tries to run to him before her partner can realize what she is up to and tag her. If she reaches IT without being tagged, then her partner becomes IT.

Touch

This is the South African name for Tag (see Game Directory).

Tree Touch

One child is IT. The other children must touch a tree to be safe. They run from tree to tree—no two children may touch the same tree—and IT tries to tag one of them in transit. Whomever he tags then becomes IT.

Wolf

The children line up on one side of the room. The other side of the room is called the Den (the "safe" area). In the middle of the room stands the Wolf. When the Wolf calls "Run," the children run to the Den. If the Wolf tags someone before he reaches the Den, then that child becomes the Wolf.

K I N G Spells King

This is a version of Red Light (see Game Directory). A line is formed, and the King stands with his back to the line, some distance away. When he calls "K I N G spells King," everyone runs forward. He turns quickly and anyone that he catches still moving is out.

Hide the Item

This is another HOT and COLD seeking game (see page 80), but several items are hidden instead of one. They are small gifts that each child who finds one may keep. The birthday child, as host, or an adult, or an older child who doesn't mind not participating in the game hides the favors and calls HOT or COLD as the children approach or move from the hiding places.

Dadel Dadel

This is the South African London Bridge (see Game Directory). The verse the children chant as they pass under the bridge is:

Dadel dadel deur die bos, Daudle daudle through the woods,
Ander kaut is lekker kos. On the other side are good things to eat.

Sailor, Sailor, Come to Work

Two sides are chosen. A safety area is marked for each team.

Side 1 says: Sailor, sailor, come to work.
Side 2 says: What's your trade?
Side 1 says: Lemonade.
Side 2 says: Do it.

Side 1 has previously decided, secretly, on the name of a trade and now writes down the first letter of the word on the ground as a clue and acts out what the trade is (musician, seamstress, woodcutter, teacher, etc.). The other side tries to guess the trade (a time limit may be set). If they guess correctly, they run to their safety area, trying to get there before anyone on the other side can catch them. Any members of Side 2 that are caught must join the Side 1 team. (This is very like My Friend Has Returned from the Orient that is played in Cuba.)

Birthday gifts of toys, clothes, and books are customary in South Africa, though occasionally relatives give a gift of money. In school, the class sings Happy Birthday to the birthday child. As in many other countries, parents make a special birthday privilege of giving the child his own way as much as possible on the day of his celebration.

Spain

THE SPECIAL treats of the Spanish birthday party are *pasteles*, which are like rich French pastries. Cakes and pastries are not usually served in Spain except on very special occasions such as birthdays. Very few Spanish homes have facilities for baking, and so pastries must be bought. The big event for the birthday child is being taken to the pastry shop to choose the *pasteles* for his birthday celebration.

Yemes de Santa Teresa
(Saint Teresa Eggs)

½ cup granulated
    sugar
¼ cup water
5 large egg yolks

Few drops lemon juice
Grated rind of ½ lemon
Confectioners' sugar
Cinnamon

Boil granulated sugar and water together until syrup begins to thicken. Beat together egg yolks, lemon juice, and grated rind. Add this in a slow stream to syrup, beating constantly. Continue cooking over moderate heat for 3 or 4 minutes, beating all the time. Remove from heat, continue to beat until mixture begins to stiffen, then place saucepan in a bowl of ice, and beat until quite stiff. Pour at once into a pan lined with waxed paper. Then, with a rubber spatula, roll up edges to form one long thin roll. Chill in refrigerator until firm, almost hard. Cut with sharp knife into 1-inch pieces, and roll these in palms of greased hands into small balls. Roll the balls in a mixture of confectioners' sugar and a pinch of cinnamon. Allow to dry out at room temperature.

Relatives and the immediate family celebrate children's birthdays in Spain. Sometimes, now, the child's friends are invited to a birthday party at home, but this is a recent development. In the past few years, the custom of sending birthday cards has also been started. Cards can be bought but very few people send them.

The Spanish house is not especially decorated for a birthday party, but the party table is set with good linen and china. Recently, in Madrid, a small number of party stores have opened and a few people, but not many, go to them and buy party hats, streamers, blowers, and balloons for a party. The guests gather to be seated around the table for refreshments. There is no birthday cake nor candles and a birthday song is not sung. In addition to the *pasteles*, sandwiches, hard candies, and cocoa are served.

Guests have been greeted with *Hola* (Hello), and they in turn wish the birthday child *Felicidades* (Congratulations, or Happy Birthday). Friends try to pull the child's ear as many times as they can as they greet him on his birthday. *Gracias* (Thank you), he says as he receives his gifts. Toys, books, clothes, school supplies, and occasionally money are the common birthday presents.

GAMES

IF OTHER children do come to the party, games are played and small prizes are given to the winners.

Hit the Bucket

For five or more players. Players form a semicircle around a bucket, standing at a distance of 8 to 12 feet. Each player has a pebble, beanbag, or some other object to throw. At the signal to throw, each player in turn tosses his missile at the bucket. Those who miss must pay a forfeit (see page 187).

Spain and Cuba Tag

Players form two lines, opposite one another, about 10 feet apart, or more. One side is called Spain, the other is called Cuba.

A player from Spain is chosen to go to Cuba. All the Cuban players hold their left hands palms up. The Spanish representative rubs his right hand over the palm of each player until he comes to the one he wants to have run after him. Instead of rubbing, he strikes this player's palm, and the Cuban player in turn chases him to the Spanish side. If the Cuban catches the Spaniard before he reaches Spain, he takes his captive back to Cuba's side. Then it is this Cuban player's turn to go to Spain and repeat the performance. The object is to get all Spain's players on Cuba's side, or vice versa.

Blindman's Buff
(see Game Directory)

Hot and Cold
(see page 80)

Hot Potato
(see Game Directory)

Sack Race
(see Game Directory)

In the villages, traditional Spanish dances are done at the birthday celebration. Spanish schools do not honor the birthday child in any particular way. He is allowed to stay up later than usual on this evening, but the biggest treat is the choosing of the *pasteles*.

Sweden

THE ENTIRE family comes to the birthday child's bed to awaken him, kiss him, and wish him *Födelsedag* (Happy Birthday) on the morning of his birthday. Friends who live nearby arrive at his house early to sing their greetings to him even before he has gotten out of bed. If they play a violin or accordion, they bring it along to accompany their song. Afterwards, they sit on the birthday child's bed and join him in a small party of hot cocoa and cookies. There is a birthday party on the child's actual birth date, but his Saint's Name Day is also celebrated with a small family party. On the 5th, 10th, 15th, 20th birthdays, and so on every five years, a larger party is given and more important gifts than usual are received.

Party invitations with an appropriate picture and

verse have been sent out in advance to ask the guests to attend the afternoon party at the birthday child's home. Relatives join the family in the evening and give their gifts at that time. Toys are customarily given to a child, though occasionally clothes or money are presented. The house is festively decorated with balloons, streamers, and the birthday cards that have arrived. Paper plates and napkins, party hats and blowers are set out for the children. Decorated loot bags filled with fruit and candy are given to each child as party favors.

Loot Bags

Decorate small white paper bags with colored pictures or designs and add glitter or sequins to make them very festive. Write "Loot Bag" across the front with a colored marking pen. Fill with various small goodies and staple tops or tie with a ribbon.

God dag (Good day) the birthday child greets his guests, and as they give him their gifts he say *Tack så mycke* (Thank you so much). Everyone is dressed in his best party clothes. A long table is set up smörgås-bord-style, and the guests help themselves to this hors-d'oeuvre buffet. Eggs, sardines, caviar, anchovies, herring, and salads are but a few of the dishes served. For us in America, a smörgåsbord buffet is ideal for teenage parties or for parties to which adults as well as youngsters are invited, as dishes can be served to suit the taste of each age group. A large dish of hot Swedish meatballs is a must at Swedish birthday parties.

Swedish Meatballs

2 pounds finely ground lean beef	4 tablespoons grated onion
1 cup fine dry bread crumbs	2 teaspoons salt
2 eggs	¼ teaspoon grated nutmeg
1⅓ cups milk	¼ teaspoon pepper

Mix all ingredients together lightly. Form into small balls, gently; make balls about 1½ inches each. Brown on all sides in hot fat, then add about ¼ cup of hot water, cover, and simmer 20 minutes. Serve hot (in a chafing dish for a buffet), with slightly thickened and well-seasoned pan gravy.

Cookies, all types of candies, and soda are part of the refreshments. *Klubba* (lollypops) are always favorites with the children. The birthday cake is a fancy molded ring made of lemon pound cake. A large candle, "The Life Light," is placed in the center of the cake ring. This candle is not blown out by the birthday child and is only extinguished, by the parents, after the birthday party is over. But smaller candles, one for each year are also placed around the top of the ring. The birthday child makes his secret wish and blows these little candles out. The cake is served with a side dish of whipped cream and strawberries that are put on it after it is sliced, and the first slice is for the birthday child. Besides the birthday cake, an ice-cream cake (thin layers of cake between thicker layers of ice cream) is also served. *Hjärtlig Gratulation På* ———(number)——— *Ars Dagen* (Hearty congratulations on your ———(number)——— years day) and flowers made of icing decorate the top of this cake.

The Swedish birthday song is sung to the child:

Jag mätte han leva,
Jag mätte han leva,
Uti 100 är ja visst ska han leva uti 100 är.

He should live a 100 years,
He should live a 100 years,
Yes, I wish that he shall live to know a 100 years.

And a photograph of the birthday child and all his friends is taken as a remembrance of the happy occasion.

174

GAMES

Fiskar
(Fishing)

This is an entertaining way to distribute party gifts to small children and is done in many different countries. The Cuban version of fishing is described on page 40, where a "well" is used to hide the gifts and the adult who pins them on the children's fishing lines; in Sweden a barrier or wall is set up to serve the same purpose.

Blind Ko
(Blind Cow)

This is Blindman's Buff (see Game Directory).

Drop the Handkerchief

This is played the same way as it is in the United States (see Game Directory), except that an object is handed to the child that IT stops in back of, rather than a handkerchief being dropped behind him.

Other familiar games that Swedish children play are checkers, hopscotch, and cowboys and Indians. Prizes of candy, fruit, or small toys are given to game winners. If the family can afford it, fireworks are set off on the evening of the birthday.

The birthday song is sung to the birthday child in school, and he brings candy to treat his classmates. Swedish children look forward to almost the complete list of traditional special birthday privileges— the birthday child is never reprimanded or spanked on this day, he is allowed to have his favorite foods at dinner, he may stay up later than usual, and he need not do any of his usual chores.

Game Directory

HERE ARE directions for well-known games often mentioned in this book, the rules for which adults may have forgotten over the years. All other games explained for various countries may be located in the Index under the general heading of Games. Suggestions for stunts for forfeit games are listed on page 187.

Blindman's Buff

IT is blindfolded. He is spun around a few times so that he loses his sense of direction. Then IT tries to catch the other players who can dodge about and tease him by making sounds near him and then ducking away when he reaches out to catch them. IT can call out "1, 2, 3, STOP," whenever he wants to, and everyone must freeze in position. Then IT can feel around to try to catch someone. Once IT catches someone, he tries to guess who it it. If IT guesses correctly, the one he caught becomes IT. If he guesses wrong the games goes on until IT does guess correctly.

Drop the Handkerchief

The children form a circle, all facing inward. IT walks behind them outside the circle holding a hankie. He drops the hankie in back of one child and runs around the outside of the circle. As soon as the other child realizes the hankie is behind him he picks it up

179

and chases IT, trying to tag him before he can reach the empty spot where he had been standing. If IT reaches the spot first without being tagged, the new child becomes IT. If the child is able to tag IT before he reaches the empty spot, IT must continue to be IT.

Hide and Seek

One child is IT. He hides his eyes at the home base and counts slowly to 25 or 50 while the other children hide. When he reaches the number he calls out, "Ready or not . . . here I come." He then proceeds to search for the others. As soon as he spots a child he calls out the child's name and they both race to touch home base first. If the other child touches first, he is safe, and IT must look for another hidden child. If IT touches first, then the other child becomes IT and the game starts again.

Hot Potato

Children sit in a circle and pass a potato (you can use a baked potato to make the game realistic) from one to another around the circle as music plays. Periodically the music stops. The child holding the potato at this moment is out. The process is repeated until only one child remains and he is the winner.

Jacks and Balls

Ten jacks and a very small ball are held in one hand. The ball is then thrown up into the air and at the same time the jacks are dropped to the floor. The ball must be caught on one bounce. The ball is then tossed up again with one hand and while it is in the air a jack is picked up with that hand. The ball must be caught on one bounce. All ten jacks are picked up this way. If the player misses, the next player gets his turn. If all the single jacks are retrieved without an error, the process is continued, this time two jacks at a time are picked up. Then three jacks at a time, etc. The winner is the one who can retrieve the highest number of jacks at a time without missing.

London Bridge

London Bridge is falling down,
Falling down,
Falling down.
London Bridge is falling down,
My fair lady.

Build it up with iron bars,
Iron bars,
Iron bars.
Build it up with iron bars,
My fair lady.

Iron bars will bend and break,
Bend and break,
Bend and break.
Iron bars will bend and break,
My fair lady.

Build it up with gold and silver,
Gold and silver,
Gold and silver.
Build it up with gold and silver,
My fair lady.

Two children form an arch with hands joined. They secretly decide which one will represent Pins and which one Needles. The other children pass under the arch singing the verses, and a child is caught at the words "My fair *lady*." He then must choose between Pins and Needles and takes his place behind the one in the arch whose side he has chosen. After the last child has chosen, there is a Tug-of-War between the two sides.

For a Tug-of-War, a separating line is drawn and the Pins stand on one side of the line behind their leader while the Needles are across the line on the other side facing them, behind their leader. A long rope is used and both sides grab the rope with the two leaders holding the center of the rope and their teams holding it behind them. At the signal, they all pull. The team that can pull the other one across the separating line first is the winner.

Musical Chairs

Set up two rows of chairs, back to back, with enough room around them so that the children can circle around them. Have one chair less than the number of players. As music plays, the children march around the chairs. At intervals, the music stops and the children must sit down on a chair (one to a seat). The child left standing is out. Now another chair is removed and the game proceeds on and on until only one chair and two players are left. The one to sit down on the last chair is the winner.

Pin the Tail on the Donkey

A large picture of a donkey with no tail is tacked up on the wall. One child at a time is blindfolded and given a paper tail marked with his name and with a pin stuck through it. The child is spun around a few times and then pushed toward the donkey. He must pin his tail at the first spot that his hand touches. The child that pins his tail nearest the spot where the tail should be wins.

Red Light

The group lines up at one end of the room. The leader, IT, stands across the room with his back to the group. The group moves forward toward the leader, but at short intervals the leader shouts "Red Light," and then turns toward them quickly. If he catches any children still moving, they are out of the game. The game continues until one of the group is able to reach and tag the leader. The leader must then turn and chase that child back to the starting line. If he tags the child, that child becomes IT. If he cannot tag the child before he reaches the starting line, then the leader must be IT all over again in the next game.

Sack Race

Each child stands in a big sack (potato sack or burlap bag), holding it up around him with his hands. All contestants line up at the starting line. At the signal all move forward in their sacks toward the finish line. The first one to cross the line is the winner.

Simon Says

Children stand in rows before a leader. The leader calls out directions for them to follow (finger on nose, hand on head, hop, etc.). The trick is that they must *not* follow the directions unless "Simon says" is said before the direction is given.

Tag

A safety base is decided upon. One child is IT; the other players scatter. IT tries to tag another player. If he can, the other player becomes IT. If he cannot, he remains IT until he can tag someone. The other players can run to the safety base but must leave the base if IT commands them to.

Treasure Hunt

Parent writes out clues and hides them in various places. One clue should lead to another. (Clue 1: "Go to kitchen." Have clue 2 hidden somewhere in kitchen. Clue 2: "Go to bedroom." Have clue 3 hidden under the bed. Clue 3: "Go to living room." Have clue 4 hidden under a sofa cushion, etc.) The children search from clue to clue until they find the treasure spot. The children can search individually, in pairs, or as a group. The treasure should be one that can be shared, if they search in a group (candy, inexpensive favors, etc.). The treasure is kept by the finder or finders. If it is a group treasure, the actual finder may receive the largest share.

List of Stunts
for Forfeit Games

1. Dance around the room with a broom for a partner.
2. Repeat rapidly BLACK BUG'S BLOOD six times.
3. Repeat rapidly SIX SICKLY SONGSTERS SIPPING CIDER three times.
4. Neigh like a horse.
5. Quack like a duck.
6. Imitate blowing bubble gum.
7. Spell your name backwards.
8. Shake hands with everyone.
9. Imitate a baby crying.
10. Pick up a hankie from the floor with your teeth.
11. Imitate a girl putting on make-up.
12. Imitate a farmer calling hogs.
13. Pretend you are a chicken.

14. Pantomine a nursery rhyme (Little Miss Muffet, Little Jack Horner, etc.).
15. Pretend you are a plane.
16. Lap up a saucer of milk without using your hands.
17. Hold one foot in your hand and hop across the room and back.
18. Hold your nose and sing a song.
19. Move your right hand up and down vertically, and at the same time move your left hand back and forth horizontally.
20. Pretend to eat a full meal (cut your meat, butter your bread, drink).

Mail Order Shopping Directory

FOOD

B. Altman & Co., P. O. Box 16, New York, New York 10016

Biscuits: This New York department store puts out the most complete booklet on biscuits (which Americans call cookies and crackers) that I have ever seen. It starts with the history of the word biscuit and gives an alphabetical listing with descriptions of more than 200 of them, suggesting uses and giving the names of the manufacturers. Biscuits from England, Scotland, Ireland, Switzerland, Belgium, Holland, Denmark, Italy, and France are available and priced by the tin, canister, drum, and packet. Everything from plain biscuits to fancy rich cookies. Varied prices.

Tea: Altman's tea guide tells the legends of tea and explains the three basic types and the terms used in their description. Important teas, their characteristics and packers are listed, and package sizes and prices are given. It also tells how to make good hot tea and good iced tea. Tea lovers will have a grand time deciding which blends to try, and it is an exciting selection to choose from for making party drinks and punches. Varied prices.

Mark Austin, 169 Kingston Road, Wimbledon, London S.W. 19, England.

191

English teas, handmade chocolates, fruit cake, petits-fours, biscuits, and candies. Varied prices.

Old Country Store, The Nashville House, Nashville, Indiana

This is one of the places to get all the old-fashioned candies. Lemon drops, red hots, cinnamon balls, licorice twists, horehound drops and sticks, rock candy on a string, gum drops; old-fashioned stick candy, from anise to wintergreen (30 flavors); old-fashioned gingerbread candy, wild forest nuts, sorghum fudge, chocolate pecan fudge, cinnamon potatoes (pieces of candy that look exactly like small potatoes, eyes and all; they are sugary and cinnamon covered), walnut cream fudge, and hickory nut fudge.

Also, old-fashioned Grandma's sunbonnets (for an old-fashioned American party), in inexpensive flowered cotton prints and various bright colors.

Ferrara Confectionary Co., 195–201 Grand Street, New York, New York 10013

Amaretti (Italian almond macaroons), *panettone* (fruit cake), *torrone* (nougat candy), syrups with natural flavors, *fourrés* (filled candies), *panforte di Siena* (spiced fruit cake). Varied prices.

Manganaro's, 488 Ninth Avenue, New York, New York 10018

Antipasto, hors d'oeuvres, pasta specialties, vegetable and fish soups, appetizers, meats, cheeses, fruits, preserves, cakes, candy. Every food for an Italian party.

Perugina, 636 Lexington Avenue, New York, New York 10022

Italian candies beautifully boxed. *Torrone* nougats, Perugina assortment, *baci* (kisses).

Paprikas Weiss, 1546 Second Avenue, New York, New York 10028

Meats, fish, cheese, nuts, spices and herbs, jams, jellies, flour, French orange-flower and rose water, true fruit syrups, herb teas, almond paste, fruit-filled candies, marzipan loaves and fruits, chocolates from Holland, imported honey candy, hard raspberry drops and jellies, golden almonds, Swiss orange slices and hard mints, German tiny peppermints, coffee beans, chocolate almonds, licorice miniatures, rock candy, burnt almonds, Italian sour lemon drops, candy-coated chocolate *pastilles,* sour fruit slices, chocolate-covered orange peels, imported licorice coins, cocoa almonds, licorice sticks, apricot-filled hard candy, crystallized Canton ginger, alphabet-shaped sour candy, chocolate Christmas-tree ornaments, *Dobosh Torte* (German seven-layer cake), Danish butter cookies. Wide variety of cake pans, cooky and cake cutters, pots, molds, tart pans, icing sets. Also, special playing cards, fortune-telling cards. Dolls of all nations, 7 inches high, with movable heads and eyes.

MUSIC

Berliner's Music Shop, 154 Fourth Avenue, New York, New York 10003

A most complete record catalogue of Folkraft records —45-rpm, 78-rpm, or 33-rpm, with music and instructions for folk and square dances. Records of music from the following countries: Germany, France, South Africa, Netherlands, Belgium, Israel, England, Denmark, Sweden, Italy, Scotland, Russia—and "Americana." There are hoedowns, instrumentals with calls, instrumental singing calls, and rounds with separate spoken calls.

Special dance syllabus records have been prepared. Number 1 for kindergarten to 6th grade; Number 2 for 7th to 9th grade; Number 3 for high school and college. Each contains folk dances, play party games, and square dances.

TOYS, NOVELTIES,
PARTY FAVORS, SUPPLIES

Azuma, 802 Lexington Avenue, New York, New York 10021

Japanese lanterns in a variety of colors and shapes, colorful decorating candles, large paper flowers, hand-painted earthenware mugs in different designs; paper-mâché nodding tiger, bright red nodding hippo, running turtle, balancing strongman, wandering woodpecker, shaking Santa; Japanese Go game, octascope.

Bazaar International, Hanover, Pennsylvania 17331

Items from all over the world. Dolls, music boxes, wood carvings, jewelry. Varied prices.

Stephen Faller, Ltd., Galway, Ireland

Irish souveniers from $1.00 up. Claddagh jewelry, tie pins and tacs, spoons, earrings, brooches, cuff links, charms in silver or gold, rosaries, key rings, rings, Connemara marble necklets.

Go Fly a Kite, Bahadur of India, 507 Fifth Avenue, New York, New York 10017

Kites of many countries (United States, India, Japan,

China, Thailand), books on kite flying, and tips for flying kites. Prices vary from 15¢ to $15.00 (for a handmade India fighter kite); Japanese kites start at 39¢.

Helen Gallagher-Foster House, 6523 North Galena Road, Peoria, Illinois 61601

Swedish tart tins, bow makers, satin ribbon, desk flag, musical cake stand (plays Happy Birthday), 21-year candle, Disneyland cake carousel, solid milk-chocolate eggs, multi-colored paper garland, honeycomb bunny centerpiece, placecard favors, bunny hand-puppet wash mit, hand-carved wooden shoes from Holland filled with wrapped chocolate eggs, 44-inch-high colorful Vinyl clown for centerpiece, party baskets, large assortment of toy favors, tablecloth to color plus crayons (48 inches square, wipes clean), Japanese polyethylene lanterns, Japanese stone-style lanterns (both lantern sets come complete with sockets, lights, and cord and bulbs), oriental silk fans, height chart on Belgian linen panel, magic re-lighting birthday candles, candle *bobêches,* pretzel press, ice-cream freezer.

Miles Kimball, Kimball Building, Oshkosh, Wisconsin 54902

Decorative butterflies, bunny puppet, huge lollypops, party baskets, side candle holders for birthday candles, re-lighting candles, treat-tray for party pops, ballerina candle holders.

Cake Decorators, Blacklick, Ohio.

Everything having to do with baking cakes or cookies; star, Christmas-tree, animal, and many other molds; decorations for sports and other hobbies, Cinderella coach complete with horses; candy-making supplies; candles of all kinds (such as special clown candles); molds for candies, candles, crafts; and innumerable party supplies and decorations *besides* cake specialties. There is everything here for all kinds of parties and holiday celebrations in addition to birthdays, and the catalogue is one of the biggest you can find anywhere.

Maid of Scandinavia Co., 3245 Raleigh Avenue, Minneapolis, Minnesota 55416

This is one of the most complete catalogues that I have even seen for party givers, and the prices are reasonable. It is my favorite. The colored pictures and variety of items will keep you spellbound for many an hour. It will become your party-giving supply reference book.

Endless variety of new and differently shaped molds and cake pans (book, bell, lamb, star, éclair, cross, football, heart, tier, zodiac, shell, tower, bunny, Santa, fruit-basket, petit-four, fruit, animal), tart pans, pretzel press, dough cutters, cooky cutters of every imaginable shape, rolling pins, party-pops tray, ice-cream and candy molds, lollypop sticks, punch ladle, napkin doll. Pastry and decorating tubes in any design ever invented, cake decorator sets, books on cake decorating; favors of all colors, types and sizes for every occasion; decorations for cake tops, cake charms, numbers and letters for decorating cake tops, cake bases, figures for cakes, musical cake bases. Cookbooks on foreign cooking and catering. Holiday decorations, ribbon, lace, paper doilies, loot bags, bow makers, bells, artificial flowers and leaves for decorating, glitter, chenille-animal decorations, trolls, miniature charms for decorating (ball and mitt, flag, camera, gun, animals, birthday cakes, phones, crowns, food etc.), miniature parasols, candle holders of all types, candle-making supplies, party cloths, cups, napkins, hats, centerpieces, candy baskets and cups, placecards, balloons and pump, noisemakers, favors, horns, masks, crowns, festoons, paper lanterns, Pin the Nose game, streamers, garlands, fringe, flag streamers, craft items, birds, Happy-Birthday plastic script, bumpy chenille, hearts, UN flags. Doll figures and animals for cake decorations, wooden athletes for cake tops, cake-top panoramas, rings, fans, special-interest cake tops ready-to-use and edible. Chocolate trains, cars, animals, money, smoke sets, bowling sets, etc. Pillar birthday candle numbered 1–21 years, Swiss funny-face lollypops, marzipan candy in shapes, large-crystal rainbow sugar (can be used as Hundreds and Thousands for an Australian party), chocolate sprills in colors.

Mark Farmer Co., 11427 San Pablo Avenue, El Cerrito, California 94532

Dolls and doll parts, kits and clothes (all reproductions of old dolls) from all over the world. Doll stands, miniature furniture, doll repair service.

Penthouse Gallery, 15 West 55th Street, New York, New York 10019

Cottons in oriental style made for children. Smocks, *happi* jackets (sizes 2–14), house-boy pants, tea-house kimonos (sizes 2–12); kimonos also in multicolored floral rayon.

Poco Imports, 2617 East Third Avenue, Denver, Colorado 80206

Mexican pig banks, Tonala animals of colorful fired clay.

H. Roth & Son, 1577 First Avenue, New York, New York 10028

Wooden napkin holders, egg cups with knitted

warmer, foreign dolls, unusual molds, chocolate Christmas-tree ornaments, raspberry syrup, fruit soup; marzipan fruits and platters of marzipan eggs, cheeses, cold cuts; design pastry roller, confectionery molds, enamel cup with painted nursery picture, lady fingers, malt candy, anise drops, honey malt drops, Tobler chocolate bars, chocolate cat tongues, foreign cookbooks. Name-Day cards in German, hand-painted wooden plates (6-inch diameter, choice of girl or boy), Black Forest weatherhouse, dolls of all countries, cake and cooky decorating sets, all types of cooky cutters, myriads of molds including lady-finger pans, doughnut maker, jelly injector, cream-roll tubes, *Dobosh Torte* pans, cooky-decorating boards, cake-decorating rollers, pig-shaped breakfast board, fortune-telling cards, beeswax, imported candies, special German cookies at Christmas only, gingerbread figures, spice drops; truffle, potato, pig, and fruit marzipan; Christmas-tree chocolate figures wrapped in colored foil.

Scottish Products, Inc., 24 East 60th Street, New York, New York 10022

Children's kilts ($15.00 up), beret tam or Tam-o'-Shanter (about $3.50), sterling silver sword kilt pins and clan crests (under $5.00). Inexpensive items: Brownie Downing ceramics, brass Toby jug, scotty paper weight, brass horse, piper or drummer in bottle, novelty bagpipe, tartan purse, historical map of Scotland or Ireland, clan map of Scotland, silk-screened and lacquered decals, dolls, books on tartans, bagpipe music. *Real* bagpipes, between $100 and $500; clothing for men, women, and children at varied prices.

F.A.O. Schwartz, 745 Fifth Avenue, New York, New York 10022

This is a wonderful toy store. Listed here are mostly ideas for birthday presents, many of them inexpensive though a few are a little extravagant. The catalogue lists items in every price range.

Unusual kites; old-fashioned ice-cream freezer, including ice-cream mix, toppings, utensils, and recipe book; *bocce* game, French bowling set, unicycle, kaleidoscope, *tamburelli;* Italian-villa doll house, peasant Swiss doll house, American doll houses of different periods (furniture and family to scale for houses available); puppet theaters (with stage and puppets), people puppets; raffia basket-making set, *origami* and *kirigami* papers, Weave-a-Basket set, weaving looms, perfume-making kit, French coloring books, table mat painting set, modern and foreign cut-out dolls, flower pops (useful barettes, bracelets, headbands with snap-on flowers), dolls, doll furniture, toy utensils, cars, trucks, games, marionettes, four-finger puppets, marionette stage, musical instruments, Kotton Kandy machine, party jokes, magic tricks, gags and puzzles, wooden puzzle sets, Coca-Cola dispenser, corn popper, hot dogger, musical jewel case with dancing ballerina, puppet mittens, Swiss skating cap, animal puppet slippers, old-fashioned cast-iron action banks, records, books; Steiff toys of varied prices, sizes, Steiff hand puppets; French puff billiards, Japanese game of Go, beautiful costumes for girls and boys, decorative fruit set (10 pieces hand-decorated with silk thread), pocket-sized puzzles, metal puzzles.

Sears, Roebuck & Co., Philadelphia, Pennsylvania 19132

Sears' *Christmas Book* is full of items that are reasonably priced and useful at any time of year. Walt Disney Wrap, ready-made bows, ribbon reels, gift paper, ribbon sets. English cookies, Scottish cookies, famous-brand teas, fruit cake, fruit-cake minatures, *Dobosh Torte* (seven-layer cake), cheese trays (from Italy, Switzerland, Norway, Denmark, Germany, Ireland, Holland, Austria), petits-fours (pastel or chocolate frostings), English chocolates and toffees, fairy-tale candy house, chocolate coins from Belgium, *piñatas* (filled with 90 candies and 20 prizes), fruit slices, glass punch bowl (4-quarts filled with 2 pounds of hard candy and 8 cups, 8 cup hangers, plastic ladle), indoor lights, outdoor lights, fancy gift boxes. Toys, games, instruments, records, books for all ages at varied prices. Costumes for children: Mary Poppins, nurse, soldier, Indian, cowboys, ballerina, evening gown, Superman, etc. Storybook string puppets: Cinderella, clown, horse, The

Beatles, troll, witch, etc. Talking hand puppets: Mr. Ed, Bugs Bunny, etc. Hand puppets and musical hand puppets, puppet theater, ventriloquist dummy, Kotton Kandy machine, pretzel machine, "lollypop factory," electric corn popper, ice-cream freezer set, Sno-Cone set, soda-fountain set, cake-baking sets, doll houses, doll-house furniture, comic plastic wigs, Saran wig (feels real), play clothes (high-heeled shoes, evening gown, bride's gown), dolls and doll clothes.

Spencer Gifts, 7A Spencer Building, Atlantic City, New Jersey 08404

Satin ribbon by the bolt, musical cake stand, re-light birthday candles, miniature fruit erasers, personalized pencils, book cake pan, rainbow ribbon, rainbow paper, bow maker, cascading drip-color candles.

Sunset House, 145 Sunset Building, Beverly Hills, California 90213

Numbers to top cake, fortune-telling cards, decorative radish cutter, quick-stick tape, everlit birthday candles, Happy Birthday musical cake plate, school photo album, Happy Birthday song girl centerpiece, brass wind chimes, bow-making machine, shell wind chimes.

The Tartan Gift Shop, 96 & 96A Princes Street, Edinburgh 2, Scotland

Miniature bagpipes (inexpensive and noisy), tartan slippers, Scottish jewelry, Scottish spoons, tartan stools, horn porridge spoons, egg spoons, spoon and pusher, horn egg cups, napkin rings, dolls, clan blazer badge, Scottish charms, map-of-Scotland towel, novelty purses, brass bell with thistle handle, pipe band in bottle, tartan address book, autograph book, poems and songs by Robert Burns, Burns Birthday Book, photo album, child's tartan apron, Highlander claymore paper knife, Scottish plastic wallets, color slides, piggy bank with map of Scotland, clan and crest map, tartan-back playing cards, piper egg timer, tartan bracelets, tartan dog collars, tartan belts, tartan knives, key chains, musical dolls, bagpipe pin cushion. Also clothing for men, women, and children at varied prices.

Index

Index

Index